ISBN 978-0-9850031-2-8

ISSN 2157-586X

THE JOURNAL OF THE BLACK CATHOLIC THEOLOGICAL SYMPOSIUM (BCTS), was founded in 2007.

MANUSCRIPTS should be submitted to the editorial board by the deadline announced at the Annual Meeting, which is also posted at http://www.bcts.org. All submissions must be formatted in Chicago Turabian style with Works Cited page and sent via electronic mail to senior editor Kimberly Flint-Hamilton: kflintha@stetson.edu, and also to editor Cecilia Moore: Cecilia.Moore@notes.udayton.edu. For examples of Chicago Turabian style, see: http://www.press.uchicago.edu/books/turabian/turabian_citatioguide.html.

The Journal of the Black Catholic Theological Symposium is composed of original articles by its members and guest contributors, and will not publish manuscripts that have been previously published elsewhere.

REVIEWS of books or films that have relevance to the Black Catholic Theological Symposium may also be submitted and will be considered for publication. Reviews originally published elsewhere will not be considered for publication.

MEMBERSHIP in the Black Catholic Theological Symposium is by invitation only. Those interested in joining the organization may review membership guidelines from Article II of the Constitution, posted on the BCTS web site: http://www.bcts.org, and contact the secretary of the BCTS, Shawnee Daniels-Sykes, SSND, at the following electronic mail address: sykess@mtmary.edu.

The opinions expressed in the articles and/or reviews published in *The Journal of the Black Catholic Theological Symposium* are those of the authors and are not necessarily the opinions of the editorial board, the organization, or the publisher.

The Journal of the Black Catholic Theological Symposium is provided to all paid members of the BCTS. Additional copies of the journal may be obtained by contacting the publisher, Steven Hamilton, of Fortuity Press, at the following electronic mail address: steven.hamilton@fortuitypress.com.

Fortuity Press
Copyright © 2013 by Fortuity Press LLC
All rights reserved.

This periodical is indexed in the ATLA Catholic Periodical and Literature Index® (CPLI®), a product of the American Theological Library Association, 300 S. Wacker Dr., Suite 2100, Chicago, IL 60606, USA. Email: atla@atla.com, www: http://www.atla.com.

No part of this volume may be reprinted or reproduced or utilized in any form by any electronic, mechanical, or other means, now known or hereafter invented, including photocopying and recording, or any information storage or retrieval system, without permission in writing from the publishers.

Printed in the United States of America.
Cover design by Steven Hamilton, Kimberly Flint-Hamilton
Cover art and photographs of The Emancipation Proclamation by Steven Hamilton
Interior design, art and photography by Kimberly Flint-Hamilton, Steven Hamilton

THE JOURNAL

OF THE

BLACK CATHOLIC THEOLOGICAL SYMPOSIUM (BCTS) VOLUME SEVEN

EDITORS

Cyprian Davis, O.S.B., Editor-in-Chief
Saint Meinrad Archabbey

Kimberly Flint-Hamilton, Senior Editor
Stetson University

Cecilia Moore, Editor
University of Dayton

Diana Hayes, Book Review Editor
Georgetown University

THE BLACK CATHOLIC THEOLOGICAL SYMPOSIUM (BCTS)

2013 OFFICERS

C. Vanessa White, Convener

Kathleen Dorsey Bellow, Associate Convener

Shawnee Daniels-Sykes, SSND, Secretary

Timone Davis, Treasurer

Cyprian Davis, OSB., Archivist

Bryan Massingale, Past Convener

THE JOURNAL OF THE BCTS

Volume Seven   2013

LETTER FROM THE EDITOR

Kimberly Flint-Hamilton   1
Seeking Freedom In 2013 That Was Promised
In 1863

REFLECTIONS

Bishop J. Terry Steib, S.V.D.   23
A Statement on the Emancipation Proclamation
150 Years Later

Kim R. Harris   25
Reflections On Freedom and the Songs of My People

ARTICLES

In Memoriam: Father Thaddeus Posey, O.F.M. Cap 29

Diane Batts Morrow   49
The Experience of the Oblate Sisters of Providence
During the Civil War Era

Joseph Flipper and Katy Leamy   73
Suffering As Glory In Hans Urs Von Balthasar and
James Cone

Sven Smith and Naseer Malik   97
The Representation of Blacks and Hispanics in
Media Depictions of the Catholic Church

BOOK REVIEWS 131

Edward J. Blum and Paul Harvey
*The Color of Christ: The Son of God and the Saga of
Race In America* (D. Hayes)

George Yancy
Christology and Whiteness: What Would Jesus Do?
(D. Hayes)

CHRONOLOGY
BCTS Annual Meetings 139

SEEKING FREEDOM IN 2013 THAT WAS PROMISED IN 1863

Kimberly Flint-Hamilton
Stetson University

No one can say that 2013 has been boring. As I write this letter, September has only just begun, yet so much has happened, so much tragedy and sadness, and not nearly enough joy. Perhaps, if we take a good, long look at these events through the lens of social justice, reaffirming our "commitment to the fundamental humanity of all persons,"[1] we can begin to make sense of them, and maybe even formulate some sort of rational response.

It started on a high note, with the inauguration of President Barack Obama for his second term of office on January 21st. Then, after barely enough time to celebrate, Pope Benedict XVI announced his resignation from the papacy, effective February 28th, citing failing health due to advanced age as his motivation – the first papal resignation in 600 years.[2] And on March 13th, the swirls of *fumata bianca* from the Sistine Chapel signaled the election of our new pontiff – Francis I of Argentina, the first Latin American pope, the first Jesuit pope, and the first non-European pope in over 1000 years.[3]

Just as we were getting to know Pope Francis, the Boston Marathon bombing grabbed our attention. On April 15th two

---

[1] Our fundamental mission – see the BCTS web site, bcts.org.
[2] The last pope to resign was Gregory XII, who was forced to step down in 1415 to end the Western Schism. He was succeeded by Pope Martin V.
[3] Pope Victor I (ca 186-198), Pope St Miltiades (311-14), and Pope St Gelasius (492-496)-were Africans. See "Reflections on African Popes," The National Black Catholic Congress, accessed September 9, 2013,
http://www.nbccongress.org/black-catholics/african-popes.asp.

The Journal of the Black Catholic Theological Symposium VII (2013): 1-22.

pressure-cooker bombs went off at the finish line of the marathon, killing three people (including an 8-year-old boy).

Less than a month later we were confronted with the May 6th rescue of three young women who had been kidnapped and held hostage for up to a decade by Ariel Castro. One of the women had borne Castro a child. Another had conceived several children but Castro had induced abortion by repeatedly beating and starving her.

Then on June 10th, jury selection began for the trial of George Zimmerman in the 'Stand Your Ground'[4] murder of 17-year old Trayvon Martin.

The case shocked America – or, at least it shocked African Americans and those who care about justice, including BCTS members. The unanimous 'not-guilty' verdict sickened and horrified us. That a young black teen could be stalked and killed while walking home from buying candy in his own neighborhood, and that his white killer, after freely admitting what he'd done, could still be acquitted – that reality causes us to reel. Is this really the year 2013, or have we somehow been transported back in time, fifty years ago, back to 1963, before the passage of the Civil Rights Act, before the March on Washington, before the election of our first African American president? This verdict was a startling reminder of how very, very far we have to go in our quest for social justice and racial equality. Our past-convener, Bryan Massingale, published his thoughts on the verdict in the *U.S. Catholic Social Justice Blog*. He described the blues that threaten to overwhelm him, saying:

---

[4] Zimmerman's lawyers cited the "Stand Your Ground" legislation when he was initially questioned but used self- defense rather than "Stand Your Ground" during the trial.

I, too, have been profiled by police officers, followed by campus safety patrols and stalked by mall security guards for doing nothing more than walking to my office, shopping for clothes, or enjoying an evening stroll. ... Living with such terror and indignity is to be expected. You don't have to wear a hoodie or sagging pants to be perceived as a threat. The very presence of a black man in any space that violates the expectations of those in authority can constitute sufficient probable cause for suspicion and danger.[5]

Juror B37 explained the verdict, in an attempt, no doubt, to ease the tension surrounding the case. She couldn't have been more wrong. Our tension only grew. Her words made us more keenly aware, not less, of the depth of racism in our society when she stated, "I think George Zimmerman is a man whose heart was in the right place. ... It just went terribly wrong." She continued by stating that, even though Zimmerman "started the ball rolling" by stalking Martin after being told by 911 operators to stay in his car: "But he wanted to do good. I think he had good in his heart, he just went overboard ... He was justified in shooting Trayvon Martin." This same juror believed that Martin "played a huge role in his [own] death. He could have ... When George confronted him, and he could have walked away and gone home. He didn't have to do whatever he did and come back and be in a fight," she said, certain that Zimmerman feared for his life.[6] Zimmerman's fear was more real to her than Martin's. Persuaded that George Zimmerman is good and just, she is just as convinced that Trayvon Martin caused his own death by standing up to Zimmerman rather than fleeing.

---

[5] Bryan Massingale, "When Profiling is 'Reasonable' Injustice Becomes Excusable", *U.S. Catholic, Social Justice Blog*, July 19, 2013, accessed August 3, 2013, http://www.uscatholic.org/blog/201307/when-profiling-%E2%80%9Creasonable%E2%80%9D-injustice-becomes-excusable-2757.

[6] Dana Ford, "George Zimmerman was 'Justified' in Shooting Trayvon Martin, Juror Says," *CNN U.S.*, July 17, 2013, accessed September 9, 2013, http://www.cnn.com/2013/07/16/us/zimmerman-juror.

Zimmerman, in other words, was acting reasonably when he stalked, threatened, fought, shot, and killed an unarmed child. Massingale's comment resonates loudly with many of us:

> We are dealing with a more or less unconscious racial bias that is manifested in the pervasive association of 'black' with criminality, in the willingness to presume the innocence of nonblacks (or, at least, to give them the benefit of the doubt), and, above all, in the inability to empathize with the plight of a black teenager confronted by an armed and 'creepy' adult. ... What is at the core of this situation, then, is the nonconscious inability of many white Americans to connect with, much less have empathy for, the experience of their fellow citizens with black skin.[7]

It was a paralyzing moment for many of us. Inspired by Bryan, however, several BCTS members shook off their shocked paralysis and shared their feelings about the verdict via the BCTS listserve. Here is a sampling of a few:

> I was just watching and reflecting on the news of the newborn prince [British Prince George Alexander Louis, born July 22, 2013] and his royal debut for the entire world to see. As exciting as this news is for me and many others, I so wish that all Black male children could be afforded this same kind of affirmation and praise upon their births. In all of this hoopla, I am recalling that years ago, when I was a labor and delivery nurse, an attending physician, upon the delivery of a Black male child, jokingly said "here is another one for the welfare rolls and the prison system." This newborn already was being racially profiled and *given a guilty verdict* and he was not in this world 2 minutes yet. I often wonder where this 24 year old is today.

---

[7] Ibid.

I hope that he is doing very well. (Shawnee Daniels-Sykes, posted July 24, 2013)

Bryan, I read your piece and also went for the comments. As usual and expected, many of the comments have a denying and defensive tone. The "declining significance of race" – the false pretense of post-racial society – in this country is the cause of the racial tragedies we face today. I am grateful to see your persistence in keeping race and racism in the front burner even as forces, both within and outside the black community, often grow tired of hearing or talking about it. I would argue that we must fight racism today with more vehemence than in the past, because racism is now a creepy, naturalized, systematized, and taken-for-granted phenomenon – a green snake under green grass can't be more dangerous! (Kwame Assenyoh, S.V.D., posted on July 23, 2013)

Greetings to all from Nigeria. I have been here since the end of June. I could not believe my ears when I heard of the [Zimmerman] verdict. …. Being black while male can be a burden especially for the younger group. This was a 17 year old kid! I am amazed at the number of people who are not prepared to allow him the chance to act like a human being – take a walk, eat ice cream, pass through any neighborhood on your way home, etc. It is even more amazing how many people who, blinded by race, cannot feel the pain of a mother and father who lost a budding 17 year-old to an utterly senseless violent act. Let us continue to reflect on the lesson of this very sad issue. May he rest in Peace. (Paulinus Odozor, posted July 21, 2013)

In 1937, Cornelius Homes, a freed man, in Winnsboro South Carolina told an interviewer from the WPA: "Although the slave question is settled, the race question will be with us always, until Jesus come the second time. It's in our politics, in our justice courts, on our highways, on our side walks, in our manners, in our religion, and in our thoughts, all the day and every day. The good [Lord] pity both sides. In the end, will it be settled by hate or by the policy of love your neighbor as you do yourself? Who knows?" Only God knows, and God waits with us in hope! (M. Shawn Copeland, posted on July 19, 2013)

To try to make sense of the senseless suffering, injustice, and tragedy of this year, we might look back 150 and 50 years. The events of 1863 and 1963 laid the groundwork for who we are today, how far we've come, and what forces we've managed to overcome. In so doing, we may also learn something about what still needs to be done.

150 years ago, President Abraham Lincoln penned the Emancipation Proclamation. It was an incredible moment in time. Lincoln had invoked his authority as Commander-in-Chief of the military to issue an executive order freeing the slaves. His intent was to create chaos in those states still in rebellion against the Union:[8]

> That on the first day of January, in the year of our Lord one thousand eight hundred and sixty-three, all persons held as slaves within any State or designated part of a State, the people whereof shall then be in rebellion against the United States, shall be then, thenceforward, and forever free; and the Executive Government of the United States, including the military and naval authority thereof, will recognize and maintain the freedom of such persons, and will do no act or acts to repress such persons, or any of them, in any efforts they may make for their actual freedom. ... And upon this

---

[8] The text of the Emancipation Proclamation can be found on the web site of the National Archives and Records Administration, http://www.archives.gov/exhibits/featured_documents/emancipation_proclamation/transcript.html (accessed August 28, 2013).

act, sincerely believed to be an act of justice, warranted by the Constitution, upon military necessity, I invoke the considerate judgment of mankind, and the gracious favor of Almighty God.

While it may be true that the Emancipation Proclamation did not, in and of itself, free any slaves, it was accepted as an official endorsement of the Abolitionist Movement and symbolized the eventual objective of the our nation's executive office to abolish slavery completely. The joy of hearing that the Proclamation had been signed was a cause for great celebration for Blacks. Lucy Davis, a slave owned by a Cape Girardeau family in Missouri who was interviewed by the Federal Writers Project in the mid-1930s, describes her mother's reaction to learning that she was free:

> When de sojers was round de neighborhood dey'd allus have me playing' round de front gate so I cud tell em when dey's comin' up the road. Den dey goes an' hides 'fore de sojers gits dar. Dey all skeer'd o' de sojers. I's skeerd too but dey say sojers won't bother little black gal. ... When de war wuz over Ole Massa Joe came in an' he say, 'Rose, you all aint slaves no mo'—You is all free as I is. Den you should a heard my mammy shout! You never heard sich shoutin' in all yo' bahn days.[9]

New Year's Eve of 1862 was celebrated as "Watch Night" by abolitionists, and New Year's Day 1863 represented the day of freedom, the end of the moral outrage that had so tainted this

---

[9] Aaron Lisec, "The Emancipation Proclamation at 150: Narratives of Soldiers and Former Slaves," *Raiders of the Lost Archives – Behind the Stacks at the Special Collections Research Center, Morris Library, SIUC*, accessed September 12, 2013, http://scrc1.wordpress.com/2013/01/08/the-emancipation-proclamation-at-150-narratives-of-soldiers-and-former-slaves/. Missouri was one of the states for whom the Emancipation Proclamation did not apply.

nation, as described by Fanny Garrison Villard on the 50th anniversary of the Proclamation:

> The recent celebrations of the Proclamations of Emancipation have brought vividly before me the "Watch Night" of New Year's Eve fifty years ago in a crowded African Church in Boston ... [w]e being the only white people present. When my father's name was mentioned we were at once given seats. The solemnity and intense excitement of the occasion were indescribably thrilling, and I almost felt as if I could hear the heart-beats of those present, as well as my own. The black preacher said, in substance: 'The President of the United States has promised that if the Confederates do not lay down their arms he will free all the slaves to-morrow. They have not laid down their arms, and to-morrow will bring freedom of the oppressed slaves. But we all know that the powers of darkness are with the President, trying to make him break his word, but we must watch and see that he does not break his word.' ... [The next day] came real exaltation of spirit with the announcement by someone from the platform that the President's proclamation was coming over the wires. Nine cheers were given for Lincoln and three for William Lloyd Garrison. I can imagine what my father's feelings were at that happy beginning of the end of slavery to which he had given more than thirty years of his life, but I know that I stood up in the gallery beside him when he received the plaudits of the audience with joy in his heart that was akin to pain. ... *The question that concerns us to-day is, more than all else, whether our duty to the liberated bondmen has been fulfilled. The answer is, alas! No. Untutored, ignorant of the meaning of liberty, they were for a long time after the war abandoned both by the North and the South (save for few exceptions) and we are still to-day repairing the harvest of our neglect.*[10]

---

[10] Fanny Garrison Villard, 1913 , "How Boston Received the Emancipation Proclamation," *AntiSlavery Literature,* accessed September 13, 2013,

A century later, Villard's words ring true. In the year 2013, we are still "repairing the harvest of neglect."

January 1, 1863 may have been a day of celebration, but the estimated 500,000 slaves held in states that weren't in rebellion – namely, Missouri, Kentucky, Maryland, Tennessee, and Delaware, and parts of Louisiana and Virginia – were not freed by the Proclamation.

> [I] designate as the States and parts of States wherein the people thereof respectively, are this day in rebellion against the United States, the following, to wit: Arkansas, Texas, Louisiana, (except the Parishes of St. Bernard, Plaquemines, Jefferson, St. John, St. Charles, St. James Ascension, Assumption, Terrebonne, Lafourche, St. Mary, St. Martin, and Orleans, including the City of New Orleans) Mississippi, Alabama, Florida, Georgia, South Carolina, North Carolina, and Virginia, (except the forty-eight counties designated as West Virginia, and also the counties of Berkley, Accomac, Northampton, Elizabeth City, York, Princess Ann, and Norfolk, including the cities of Norfolk and Portsmouth[)], and which excepted parts, are for the present, left precisely as if this proclamation were not issued. And by virtue of the power, and for the purpose aforesaid, I do order and declare that all persons held as slaves within said designated States, and parts of States, are, and henceforward shall be free; and that the Executive government of the United States, including the military and naval authorities thereof, will recognize and maintain the freedom of said persons.[11]

---

http://antislavery.eserver.org/legacies/how-boston-received-the-emancipation-proclamation [emphasis added].
[11] From the Emancipation Proclamation, pages 1-2.

Slavery was not declared illegal in our nation until the Thirteenth Amendment was passed on December 18, 1865. We can only imagine the devastation felt by the slaves who discovered that the Proclamation did not apply to them. Consider this letter written to President Lincoln by Annie Davis, a slave held in Maryland which was not in rebellion:

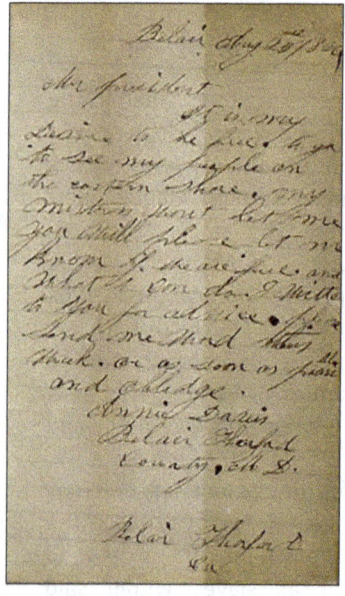

Mr. President

It is my Desire to be free. To go to see my people on the eastern shore. My mistress wont let me. You will please let me know if we are free. And what I can do. I write to you for advice. Please send me word this week. Or as soon as possible, and oblidge.

Annie Davis

Figure 1: Annie Davis' Letter[12]

Viewed through the lens of social justice, the sentiment of the Emancipation Proclamation is flawed and inadequate. But it remains a testament to the tenacious spirit of our ancestors, who

---

[12] A'Lella Bundles, "Slave's Letter Reveals Pace of Freedom, Your Take: Annie Davis' plea speaks volumes on the 150th birthday of the Emancipation Proclamation," *MSNBC's The Root*, January 1, 2013, accessed September 13, 2013, http://www.theroot.com/views/slaves-letter-reveals-pace-freedom; Image taken from "Letter to President Lincoln from Annie Davis," *National Archives, Docs Teach*, accessed September 13, 2013, http://docsteach.org/activities/7678/print.

took that germ of goodness and nurtured it to full blossoming, to the end of slavery, to full participation in our democracy. And so the Emancipation Proclamation – clearly a brilliant military stratagem and not the manifestation of any passion Lincoln may have had for our freedom – remains the most significant document in American history. Those five handwritten pages are among the most important words ever written. Whatever their intent, they served to crystalize a burning passion for an end to the ultimate dehumanization in all those who cared about justice – slaves and free, black and white. There can be no more powerful symbol of freedom for the United States.

This year marks another great anniversary – the 1963 March on Washington. It was during this historic moment that the Reverend Martin Luther King, Jr., gave his famous "I Have A Dream" speech to the estimated 250,000 people gathered at the National Mall. Today, fifty years later, it's hard to explain to our students how charged the environment had become, how our ancestors were forced to live like second-class citizens or risk their very lives, how courageous the "Freedom Riders" were for simply insisting on being served food and drink in the South. So many died during those battles, risking everything just so that their descendants might have the gift of simple human dignity.

Ken Howard,[13] a Howard University student at the time who would later become an administrator with the D.C. Department of Education, tries to explain what it was like on that sweltering August 28 day: "It's difficult for someone these days to understand what it was like, to suddenly have a ray of light in the dark. That's really what it was like." He continues:

---

[13] Michael Fletcher, "A Change Is Gonna Come" *Smithsonian* 44[4] (July-August 2013): 41.

> In May 1963, Bull Connor with the dogs and fire hoses, turning them on people, front-page news. And then in June, that summer, you have Medgar Evers shot down in the South, and his body actually on view on 14th Street at a church in D.C. So you had a group of individuals who had been not just oppressed, but discriminated against and killed because of their color. The March on Washington symbolized a rising up, if you will, of people who were saying enough is enough.[14]

A few weeks ago, I was sipping coffee in my living room waiting for the 5:00 AM news before heading out to my university, when a PBS special called *The March* began. I was so captivated by the video footage of that historic day that I never heard the morning news (and I was almost late for an early morning meeting!). I looked for Catholic nuns in habits and priests in their collars – to my relief I did see a few, and I know that there were many in attendance that day (though perhaps there should have been more). It was an excellent documentary. Toward the end, I noticed a sign carried by a woman which read, "We Seek Freedom in 1963 That Was Promised in 1863." How far have we come, fifty years later? We have an African American president, which would have been unimaginable then. When Barack Obama was elected President in 2008, we felt like Lucy Davis and her mother did 150 years ago, "You never heard sich shoutin' in all yo' bahn days!" Yet, we are still abandoned, as Fanny Garrison Villard observed a century ago, "they were for a long time after the war abandoned both by the North and the South (save for few exceptions) and we are still to-day repairing the harvest of our neglect." President Obama has received more death threats against himself and his family than any other president. A glance through the U.S. Census

---

[14] Ibid.

reveals how far we have to go before we can claim to have achieved equality.[15]

- 26% of Blacks live in poverty compared with 9.9% of those who are White, non-Hispanic (2007-2011)
- 37% of Black children live in poverty – making Black children the most impoverished of all racial/ethnic groups (2009)
- The average per-capita income for Blacks is $18,135, compared with $28,034 for Whites (and $15,063 for Hispanics; 2009)
- Blacks make up 38% of the prison population convicted of violent crime, and 39% of the jail population (2009)
- 44% of the prison population under a sentence of death are "Blacks and other" (2009)

We commemorate another important anniversary this year. In 1963, the second session of the Second Vatican Council was convened. Vatican II marked the beginning of a new era for the Church. The sixteen documents that resulted from the Council gave new shape, new vision, and new focus for the Catholic Church. Two documents were promulgated by Pope Paul VI in 1963:

- *Constitution on Sacred Liturgy* transformed the liturgy and advocated translation from Latin into vernacular languages.[16]

---

[15] *United States Census Bureau*, http://www.census.gov/ (accessed 13 September 2013).

- *Decree on Means of Social Communication* acknowledged the role of the media in our changing world and the good it can serve in informing and educating us. It also reminded us of our responsibilities in producing, using, and responding to media as Catholics and as parents and citizens.[17]

The most significant of the documents, however, wasn't released until the following year. *Dogmatic Constitution on the Church – Lumen Gentium*[18] was promulgated by Pope Paul VI in 1964. *Lumen Gentium*, "light of the nations," describes its revolutionary message – that salvation is not limited to Catholics only, but includes *all* people of God regardless of faith tradition. Here too we see the Church promoting a message of racial justice and equality in following paragraph:

> 32. By divine institution Holy Church is ordered and governed with a wonderful diversity. "For just as in one body we have many members, yet all the members have not the same function, so we, the many, are one body in Christ, but severally members one of another." Therefore, the chosen People of God is one: "one Lord, one faith, one baptism;" sharing a common dignity as members from their regeneration in Christ, having the same filial grace and the same vocation to perfection; possessing in common one salvation, one hope and one undivided charity. *There is,*

---

[16] "Constitution on Sacred Liturgy," *II Vatican Council, October 11, 1962 – December 8, 1965,* accessed September 13, 2013, http://www.cin.org/v2litur.html.

[17] "Decree on Means of Social Communication," *II Vatican Council, October 11, 1962 – December 8, 1965,* accessed September 14, 2013, http://stjosef.at/council/.

[18] "Dogmatic Constitution on the Church – Lumen Gentium," *II Vatican Council, October 11, 1962 – December 8, 1965,* accessed September 14, 2013, http://www.cin.org/v2church.html.

therefore, in Christ and in the Church no inequality on the basis of race or nationality, social condition or sex, because "there is neither Jew nor Greek: there is neither bond nor free: there is neither male nor female. For you are all 'one' in Christ Jesus."[19]

Our present is shaped by our past. In some cases, the injustices and oppressions of the past leech into our present, tainting and poisoning our communities. There are still too many George Zimmermans and Jurors 37B, too many innocent victims like Trayvon Martin who suffer from our society's failure to see past the veil of their own ethnocentrisms, who don't try to dream the dream of justice. Will it take yet another century before we can begin to realize it?

---

[19] Ibid., emphasis added.

This year, the BCTS suffered the loss of two of our brothers. Moses Anderson, S.S.E. (1928-2013), retired Auxiliary Bishop of Detroit from 1982-2003, passed away on January 1st of this year. He was the first African-American bishop of Detroit. Anderson was a charter member of the BCTS and attended the 1978 meeting in Baltimore. Later, he contributed to *Theology: A Portrait in Black*.[20]

Figure 2: Bishop Moses Anderson, S.S.E. (1928-2013)

---

[20] Moses Anderson, S.S.E., "Self-Identity – A Christian Concept," *Theology: A Portrait in Black* (Philadelphia: The Capuchin Press, 1980): 39-51.

Figure 3: Bishop Moses B. Anderson's Coat of Arms

[His] *"coat of arms includes symbols of his aspirations in ministry as well as his personal history.*

The shield most prominently contains a cross made of Kente cloth, which represents Anderson's African heritage and faith. The cross is covered with three golden rings like those that appear on the coat of arms of St. Edmund of Canterbury, a symbol of the Holy Trinity.

The bottom left corner includes an image of the Edmund Pettus Bridge in Selma, Ala. where Anderson was born. The bridge is a symbol of the Civil Rights movement.

The bottom right corner contains a pyramid and the tablets of the Ten Commandments, which is another symbol of Anderson heritage combined with a symbol of his faith.

The number of tassels draped alongside the shield, six, is representative of Anderson's title as bishop.

The motto below the shield—Unity in Diversity—is representative of Anderson's hope for a diverse world."[21]

---

[21] Bishop Anderson's portrait and coat of arms content used with permission of the Archdiocese of Detroit. http://www.aod.org/our-archdiocese/meet-our-bishops/retired-bishops/bishop-moses-anderson/.

We also lost a founder, Dr. Fr. Thaddeus J. Posey, O.F.M. Cap (1944-2013). Fr. Thaddeus brought together the group of scholars and graduate students who were to become the Black Catholic Theological Symposium. He was also the founding director of the Institute for Black Catholic Studies in New Orleans. We owe Fr. Thaddeus a great debt – he is honored in this volume with an *In Memoriam* essay.

Figure 4: Father Thaddeus Posey, O.F.M. Cap (1944-2013)

Additionally, in this volume are reflections on this special anniversary by Bishop James Terry Steib, S.V.D., Bishop of Memphis, Tennessee, and by BCTS member Kim Harris. We also feature three important articles: Diane Batts Morrow's *The Experience of the Oblate Sisters of Providence during the Civil War Era*, Joseph Flipper's *Suffering As Glory In Hans Urs Von Balthasar And James Cone*, and Sven Smith's and Naseer Malik's *The Representation of Blacks and Hispanics in Media Depictions of The Catholic Church*. Finally, Book Review Editor Diana Hayes offers her insights on two 2012 books, *The Color of Christ: The Son of God and the Saga of Race in America* by Edward J. Blum and Paul Harvey, and *Christology and Whiteness: What Would Jesus Do?*, edited by George Yancy. We may not have realized our goal of justice and equality, but in asking the difficult questions about our traditions and customs, learning more about the successes of our ancestors, and scrutinizing our own practices and those of the media, perhaps we are moving in the right direction.

WORKS CITED

Anderson, Moses, S.S.E., "Self-Identity – A Christian Concept." *Theology: A Portrait in Black* (Philadelphia: The Capuchin Press, 1980): 39-51.

Archdiocese of Detroit. "Bishop Moses Anderson > Coat of Arms." Accessed September 17, 2013. http://www.aod.org/our-archdiocese/meet-our-bishops/retired-bishops/bishop-moses-anderson/coat-of-arms/.

Bundles, A'Lelia. "Slave's Letter Reveals Pace of Freedom, Your Take: Annie Davis' Plea Speaks Volumes on the 150th Birthday of the Emancipation Proclamation." *MSNBC's The Root*, January 1, 2013. Accessed September 13, 2013. http://www.theroot.com/views/slaves-letter-reveals-pace-freedom.

Fletcher, Michael. "A Change Is Gonna Come." *Smithsonian* 44[4] (July-August 2013): 38-49.

Ford, Dana. "George Zimmerman was 'Justified' in Shooting Trayvon Martin, Juror Says." *CNN U.S.*, July 17, 2013. Accessed September 9, 2013. http://www.cnn.com/2013/07/16/us/zimmerman-juror.

II Vatican Council, October 11, 1962 – December 8, 1965. "Constitution on Sacred Liturgy." Accessed September 13, 2013. http://www.cin.org/v2litur.html.

II Vatican Council, October 11, 1962– December 8, 1965. "Decree on Means of Social Communication." Accessed September 14, 2013. http://stjosef.at/council/.

II Vatican Council, October 11, 1962 – December 8, 1965. "Dogmatic Constitution on the Church – *Lumen Gentium.*" Accessed September 14, 2013. http://www.cin.org/v2church.html.

Lisec, Aaron. "The Emancipation Proclamation at 150: Narratives of Soldiers and Former Slaves." *Raiders of the Lost Archives – Behind the Stacks at the Special Collections Research Center, Morris Library, SIUC.* Accessed September 12, 2013. http://scrc1.wordpress.com/2013/01/08/the-emancipation-proclamation-at-150-narratives-of-soldiers-and-former-slaves/.

Massingale, Bryan. "When Profiling is 'Reasonable' Injustice Becomes Excusable." *U.S. Catholic, Social Justice Blog,* July 19, 2013. Accessed August 3, 2013. http://www.uscatholic.org/blog/201307/when-profiling-%E2%80%9Creasonable%E2%80%9D-injustice-becomes-excusable-2757.

National Archives and Records. "Emancipation Proclamation." Accessed August 28, 2013. http://www.archives.gov/exhibits/featured_documents/emancipation_proclamation/transcript.html.

National Archives, Docs Teach. "Letter to President Lincoln from Annie Davis." Accessed September 13, 2013. http://docsteach.org/activities/7678/print.

The National Black Catholic Congress. "Reflections on African Popes." Accessed September 9, 2013. http://www.nbccongress.org/black-catholics/african-popes.asp.

United States Census Bureau. Accessed September 13, 2013. http://www.census.gov/.

Villard, Fanny Garrison. 1913. "How Boston Received the Emancipation Proclamation." *AntiSlavery Literature.* Accessed September 13, 2013. http://antislavery.eserver.org/legacies/how-boston-received-the-emancipation-proclamation.

A STATEMENT ON THE EMANCIPATION PROCLAMATION – 150 YEARS LATER

Most Reverend J. Terry Steib, S.V.D.
Bishop of Memphis in Tennessee

As a young lad growing up in the State of Louisiana, I would never have dreamed that an African American man would become the President of the United States of America. I would have been amazed to think that the Catholic Archbishop of Atlanta, Georgia – at one time the soul of the Confederacy – would be led, not just once, but twice by African American bishops. That a Secretary of State would be an African American man and later an African American woman would have seemed impossible to this young African American lad from the sugarcane fields of Louisiana.

But, I have seen all these astonishing events take place in my lifetime. So, 150 years after the Emancipation Proclamation, we are grateful for these and other accomplishments by African Americans. We are grateful for accomplishments which come as a result of a strong commitment to justice and equality as defined by our Catholic tradition.

And more is yet to be accomplished. One hundred and fifty years after the Emancipation Proclamation, we in the United States continue to struggle with racism, with poverty, and with poor education. As a Church, we Catholics continue to preach from the example of Jesus Christ who proclaimed that ALL are sons and daughters of an Almighty God, that ALL are sisters and brothers to one another as children of an everlasting God, and that ALL are equal, worthwhile and dignified by a gracious God. We continue to preach that Good News of Jesus telling us that ours is a God of love and that we all must love one another.

Just as the young patriots who formed our Constitution wrangled with the hypocrisy of slavery, so too must we continue to struggle with its plaguing results. One hundred and fifty years later, it still is our task as Americans to uphold justice and dignity as bestowed and promised by our God.

REFLECTIONS ON FREEDOM AND THE SONGS OF MY PEOPLE

Kim R. Harris

Through this week of commemorating the 1963 March on Washington for Jobs and Freedom, I am touched by many historic sounds and images. Fifty years ago I was six years old, trying to comprehend how my father, Clifford Richards Jr. was participating in a non-violent march. Could it be that he would refuse to hit back if someone hit him first? Now as an adult, grateful for his service and determination, I watch the black and white grainy television images. Like I did as a child, I still try to catch a glimpse of my father in that crowd of 250,000.

As a Black Catholic Womanist seeing the footage, I lament that during the "formal" program Daisy Bates, the only female speaker, received literally one minute of time. Yet, I rejoice that the "Tribute to Negro Women Fighters for Freedom" included a Black Catholic woman, student leader, Freedom Ride coordinator and courageous participant, Diane Nash Bevel. I hear the pointed speech of twenty-three year old SNCC founder and chairperson, John Lewis. I also see an interview with Congressman Lewis many years after the march, now in high definition. Still mourning the lives of those who died for freedom, he gently touches the chiseled name of Black Catholic Civil Rights martyr James Earl Chaney, on the memorial in Montgomery, Alabama.

Along with these many images, I hear what Sr. Thea called the "songs of our people," spirituals and freedom songs. The SNCC Freedom Singers stand at the podium during the march, singing "We Shall Not Be Moved." Len Chandler leads folk music luminaries in "Keep Your Eyes On The Prize." Sign-waving young people in the crowd sing their own Motown inspired version of "Woke Up This Morning With My Mind Stayed On Freedom." During their song, an announcer brings Marian Anderson to the podium. She sings and prays "He's Got The Whole World In His Hands." Odetta excites the crowd with "I'm On My Way to Freedom Land" just after Joan Baez sings "We Shall Overcome" and "Oh Freedom Over Me." Famed trio, Peter, Paul and Mary sing "Blowing in the Wind," anecdotally based by singer-songwriter Bob Dylan on the spiritual "Many Thousand Go (No More Auction Block For Me)."

Watching these song leaders and performers prime the atmosphere, I reflect that just as the actions of Black Catholics strengthened the warp and weave of the modern Civil Rights Movement, so too, we are deeply embedded in the origins of this music of faith and freedom. We are not latecomers to the "songs of our people." They belong to us, not only by memory through our grandparents, by adoption in our post Vatican II churches or by Protestant conversions to our faith tradition. They are ours by virtue of the "blood, tears, toil and sweat" of our brothers and sisters in the Movement.

These songs, in their form as spirituals, also belong to us through the composition, creativity, and courage of our Black Catholic ancestors who fought for emancipation from slavery. Black Catholic Civil War soldiers and presumably the women working and traveling with them, creating and reshaping spirituals in their interfaith regiment, the 1st Regiment South Carolina Volunteer Infantry [African Descent], declared their freedom singing "No More Auction Block For Me." They marched to the strains of "Hail Mary" as they called for more valiant soldiers to help them bear the cross. They admonished sinners and cried "holy, holy" as they told of the woman Mary who had one Son. They joined their voices with their brothers and sisters who endured jail for singing "We'll Soon Be Free" at the outbreak of the rebellion. They professed their faith in song.

> He have been wid us, Jesus. He still wid us, Jesus.
> He will be wid us Jesus. Be wid us to the end.

These are songs of the formerly enslaved that fought for their dream of freedom. These are songs that also inspired the concept and even formed the content of Civil Rights Movement freedom songs.

Through this week of commemorations, I remembered, more convincingly, that the music and the movements for emancipation and civil rights are ours as Black Catholics, as well as they belong to our brothers and sisters in racial and cultural heritage, in religious tradition and in allied struggle. To read of Black Catholic bravery is for me to continue growing in knowledge. To find Black Catholic exploits in the struggle is for me to grow in justified pride. To sing the songs of our people is for me, for us, to become more deeply who we authentically and truly are.

IN MEMORIAM
FATHER THADDEUS POSEY, O.F.M. Cap.

Kimberly Flint-Hamilton
Stetson University

Cecilia Moore
University of Dayton

Saturday September 17th, 2011 – the day was windy and overcast, though the blustery pre-autumn weather did not stop people from strolling along the Daytona Beach seashore, playing ball, surfing, and otherwise enjoying the day. Fr. Thaddeus had flown in the previous evening from his home at the St. Fidelis Friary in Victoria, Kansas, a trip that can take upwards of 12 hours with at least two layovers. Though tired, and still suffering from the discomforts of recent surgery to treat his persistent cancer, Fr. Thaddeus hadn't minded the trip. He told us that he loved to fly, and that the time spent in the air provided a space for quiet contemplation. His small hotel room faced the beach, which offered a stunning view of the Atlantic Ocean. Ironically, the beauty of the ocean view was a complicating factor for our interview, for it created lighting problems as we attempted to video-record our talk. All in all, however, our team of four – Thaddeus Posey, O.F.M. Cap, Cecilia Moore, Kimberly Flint-Hamilton, and Steve Hamilton – enjoyed a morning and afternoon of conversation, as Fr. Thaddeus recalled events from his life, both happy and sad, about his family, education, vocation, and life in the military. Fr. Thaddeus was the fourth person interviewed for the BCTS Oral History Project. His passing is a reminder of how critical this project is for us as a community of teachers and scholars. The chance to tell our own stories, in our own words, and to share those stories with others who strive for justice and equality is what the project is all about. What emerged from our nearly four-hour interview was a picture of Fr. Thaddeus in his diverse and complex roles – as son, as priest, as charter member of the BCTS and co-founder of the IBCS, as educator, and as army chaplain.

Although the Posey family has deep roots in Leonardtown, Maryland, Fr. Thaddeus – born John William Posey, Jr. – was born and raised in Washington, D.C. Thaddeus was the elder child of John William Posey, Sr. (1919-1989) and Teresa Braxton Posey (1922-2005) and their younger child was a daughter, Rita T. Posey Moore.

> So we come from St. Mary's County, [Maryland,] Leonardtown of course being a central point. It's kind of funny when you think about it ... I went to high school at Archbishop Carroll. ... The majority of the blacks there were Southern Maryland rooted. The other joke of it is most of us were related in some ways to somebody there. ... You can name the major families, you think about the Braxtons, the Procters, the Meriwethers, the Madisons, the Masons, all of those folks were people who, if you went back to Southern Maryland, lived down the street or down the road, or on the farm behind us, that kind of thing, so it was that kind of crowd. These folks had either moved to D.C. to old St. Augustine's which was our original parish, or to St. Cyprian's over on East Capital area.

Thaddeus' parents were leaders in the Washington black Catholic community. One of their goals was parish integration. To that end, they started the Home Visit Program, inviting white couples into their home in an effort to begin breaking down cultural barriers. They welcomed open conversation, questions, and reflection. At its zenith more than 400 people were active in this program. As a result of this and other initiatives, Fr. Thaddeus' parents were named Catholic Couple of the Year by the Archdiocese of Washington in 1965. They later received the highest honor awarded by the papacy to the laity, the Papal Award, *Pro Ecclesia et Pontifice,* in 1973.

Figure 1: Fr. Thaddeus with Picture of Parents

Figure 2: John and Teresa Posey

Teresa Posey's career with the DC public school system spanned 36 years. She started as an elementary school teacher, then advanced to the position of principal of Maury Elementary School, the laboratory school for the University of District of Columbia. Ultimately she was Regional Superintendent of Schools for the D.C. public school system. John William Posey, Sr. was a career military man, ultimately reaching the rank of Lieutenant Colonel in the United States Army. Together, John and Teresa Posey created a home environment that made the life of the mind and nurturing of the soul its centerpiece, bolstered with a sense of commitment to parish community and self-discipline.

Figure 3: The Posey Family, c. 1964
John William Posey Sr., John William Posey Jr., Teresa Braxton Posey, and Rita Posey

Fr. Thaddeus began his formal education at Maury Elementary School and transferred to St. Gabriel's Elementary when his family moved in 1955. He attended Archbishop Carroll High School, and entered St. Fidelis College in 1961, ultimately completing his bachelor's degree in philosophy. From there he earned a master's degree in religious education from Capuchin College in Washington in 1970. He was ordained in 1971.

Figure 4: John William Posey Jr., about age 6
Notice the tie monogrammed with the letter "J"

Thaddeus was the sixth religious in his family. He joined five older cousins whose communities included the Oblate Sisters of Providence, the Sisters of the Holy Family, and the Carmelites.

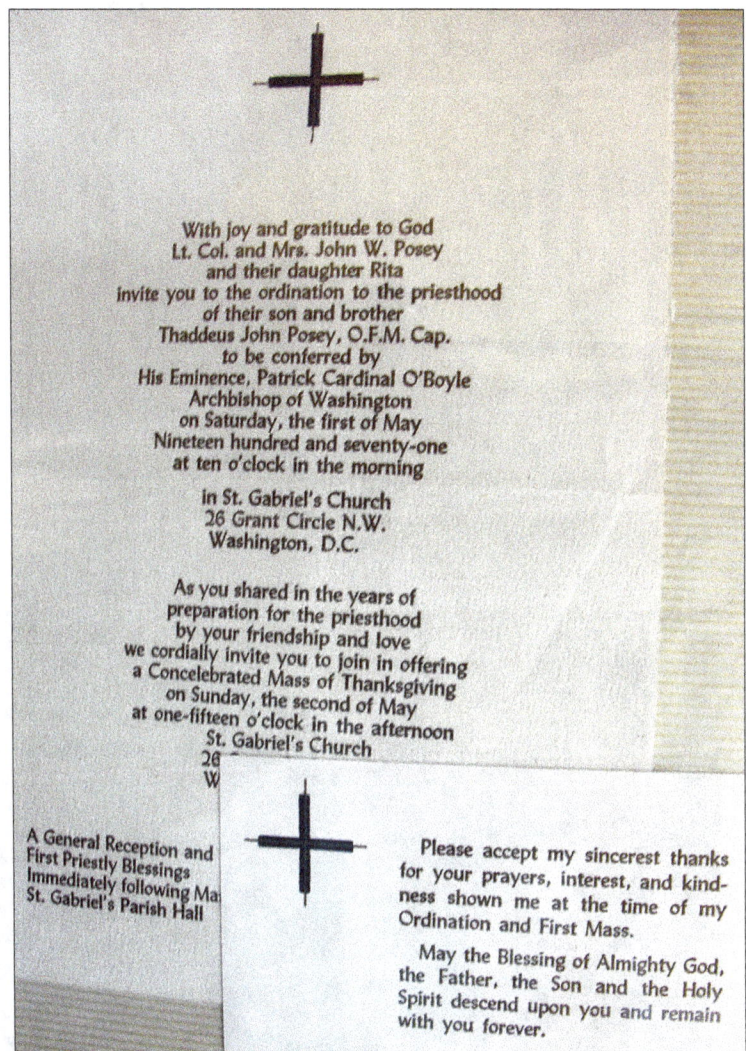

Figure 5: Announcement of Reception for Thaddeus' Ordination

Figure 6: Newly-ordained Fr. Thaddeus, his parents John and Teresa, and sister Rita

Figure 7: Fr. Thaddeus Celebrating First Mass

In Memoriam: Father Thaddeus Posey, O.F.M. Cap.

Figure 8: Young Father Thaddeus

Following his ordination, Thaddeus was assigned as a counselor to his alma mater, Archbishop Carroll High School. He stayed for nearly three years. From there he was transferred to Denver, Colorado, as assistant pastor of Annunciation Church and teacher/counselor at Bishop Machebeuf High School and chaplain of the juvenile detention center.

Thaddeus was the first African American priest at Annunciation Church. The nearly all-white congregation found his presence so unusual that some mothers brought their children specifically to meet him.[1] In a 1973 interview for *The Denver Post*, Thaddeus commented on the obstacles encountered by those who fight for social justice:

---

[1] Virginia Culver, "People Watch Black Priest," *The Denver Post*, Friday December 21st, 1973.

> It seems anyone interested in social justice is branded a supermilitant nowadays. They're considered just another radical. Maybe people are tired, or maybe they're not aware of the situation. Some think that we've already been through the civil rights struggle and it's all over. But it's not. We have an obligation to continue the struggle for Chicanos, Indians and blacks.[2]

Thaddeus did most of the cooking for his Denver friary. It wasn't uncommon, however, for the friars to offer food from their own pantries to the poor who lived in the neighborhood.

> *I did ... all the cooking for our house. [One day] I made dirty rice. And I had worked on my dirty rice, you know, you boil those livers and guts and you chop them up and then you put in your onion, and you do all of this and then folded it into the rice. And I had it kind of sitting on the edge of the stove cooling. A lady from Louisiana three doors down came by the back and ... it was summer so the back door was open. She smells dirty rice, came in, Ben said, right, take it if you want it. I was ready to kill him. I came home and my dirty rice was gone! And the lady, Emma came up to thank me ... but on the other hand that gave them something for dinner.*

While in Denver, Thaddeus rented space in a gymnasium for the youth he counseled. Not only did this help some children develop skills – even allowing some to earn certification in water safety to qualify for summer jobs as lifeguards – it also afforded him the opportunity to develop his own expertise in martial arts. As a child, he had begun learning martial arts with his father, and he

---

[2] Ibid.

continued to practice through much of his adult life. The time Thaddeus spent with martial arts allowed him to focus and reflect on his life.

> Well, for a lot of folks this gave them a chance, you know ... in this busy, busy world with everything running, to be quiet. .. Turn the noise off, everything, be quiet. [T]hey used put a rose in a vase in front of you [and say], study the rose. And well after three minutes, somebody [would start to talk] ... no, no, study the rose. And you move to it. It helps people to see and experience a different dimension of life than the hustle bustle that you can get into, plus you have a chance to develop physically, but you see that in the different light if you have a good person training you. That is not the external force to beat folks up. It's a way of life, and therefore that makes a difference.

Thaddeus had a passion for airplanes and flying from the time he was a child. This passion eventually led him to the military. With encouragement from his father, he joined the U.S. Army Reserves Chaplaincy in 1977. He served for 29 years before retiring in 2007.

> [B]efore I went to seminary I was accepted at the Air Force Academy, though I went to the seminary. But Air Force ... planes and all of that ... I used to make model planes and all, and that's my world, I still love flying. Sitting on the plane yesterday coming in I was saying, gosh do I love this.

The opening of the Capuchin's Mid-America province in 1977 prompted another move for Thaddeus, this time to Kansas City, Missouri. He served his religious community as Provincial Secretary and Treasurer while serving his country as Assistant Chaplain in the Readiness Command. He also taught at Cardinal Ritter College

Preparatory school in St. Louis. It was during this time that the first meeting of the BCTS at the Motherhouse of the Oblate Sisters of Providence took place in 1978, and the Institute for Black Catholic Studies (IBCS) began at Xavier University in New Orleans in 1980. Thaddeus was founding director of the IBCS, continued in this role until 1991. During this time he taught at St. Louis University and Cardinal Ritter Preparatory School in St. Louis. He also began doctoral studies, ultimately completing his Ph.D. in Historical Theology in 1993. He then joined the faculty of the University of St. Thomas in Minnesota, and, in addition to his regular teaching duties, taught extension courses in Ghana on African Christianity.[3] Thaddeus retired from the University of St. Thomas in 2006. He was eventually stationed at Walter Reed Army Medical Hospital in Washington, D.C., and earned the rank of Colonel before retiring in 2007.

Thaddeus reflected on the need for Catholic chaplains, especially during the turbulent years of the Iraq and Afghan wars.

> *This is the first war people can talk about [the wars in Iraq and Afghanistan] that they were in and they didn't get to see a priest, you know it used to be you could say 10 masses on a Sunday if you have that much time, but [now] people usually say three, four masses on a Sunday because you will move from one post to the next one to the next one, or you ended up saying mass all through the week in a different post, that's the only time you could get there. There are guys who didn't see [a priest at all], or maybe saw the priest once, the entire time, you know, the 12 to 18 months that they spent in Iraq. ... We're are lucky if there are 60 diocesan priests in the Army right now, 60 ... Army logistics*

---

[3] *Denver Post Obituaries*, "Fr. Thaddeus Posey O.F.M. Cap.," August 10, 2013, accessed September 6, 2013,
http://www.legacy.com/guestbooks/denverpost/guestbook.aspx?n=thaddeus-posey&pid=166348047#sthash.RHsrPQp2.dpbs.

says we need 240 priests, there are not even 100. ... If you just send one from every diocese, do you realize you would fill that up. And I don't care which, you know, Army, Navy, Air Force, I don't care where you go. But just one would make a difference.

Upon his retirement from the military, Thaddeus was honored with the Legion of Merit Award. The certificate he received reads as follows:

> The Legion of Merit Award is presented to Chaplain Colonel Thaddeus J. Posey for extraordinary meritorious service while serving in key leadership positions spanning over twenty-nine years, culminating as Chaplain, 88th Regional Readiness Command. His unwavering dedication, inspiring loyalty and consistently outstanding performance of duty were key to the successful completion of numerous critical missions during a time of ... national crisis. Chaplain Posey's exceptional professionalism, compassionate Chaplain care and superior leadership skills were evident in all missions completed resulting in the increased readiness throughout the entire command. Upon retirement, Chaplain Posey is recognized for exemplary service in the finest traditions of the United States Army.[4]

Thaddeus was also presented with the Presidential Certificate of Appreciation:

> For service in the Armed Forces of the United States, Chaplain Thaddeus J. Posey, I extend to you my personal thanks and sincere appreciation for your honorable service

---

[4] *The Provincial Porter, A Newsletter of the Capuchin Province of Mid-America*, issue 139 (April 2007): 5, accessed August 10, 2013, www.capuchins.org.

to our nation. *You helped to maintain the security of the United States of America with a devotion to duty that is in keeping with the proud tradition of our Armed Forces. I honor your service and respect the commitment and loyalty you displayed over the years. My best wishes to you for happiness and success in the future. (signed) George W. Bush, Commander in Chief.*[5]

Throughout our interview Thaddeus kept returning to the power of education to change lives. Thaddeus was inspired and motivated by the fact that our people fought and died to have an opportunity for education. He truly believed that education is our ticket to a better life, to freedom, and to justice.

Education is opportunity. A hundred years ago that's what our people were fighting for. We don't give them [children] the opportunity, we don't challenge them to know things. ... If they can get out here and memorize all these songs, and all this rap and everything else, why can't they memorize their times table? We've got teachers who don't want to ask them to do that.

Committed to the notion that real education has the power to truly transform, Thaddeus passionately supported the liberal arts because of their power to humanize, to inspire, and to helping people to grow.

A liberal arts education ... exposes the mind and the spirit to the creativity of the world. [Education] helps you to dream, to think, to look out and see.

---

[5] Ibid.

Thaddeus' impact on Black Catholic life, scholarship and institutions was been profound. He was an active member of the National Black Catholic Clergy Caucus from its inception until 1989. He was a charter member of the BCTS and coordinated its first meeting in 1978, and was also the driving force for the creation of the Institute for Black Catholic Studies in 1980, serving as director and interim director for many years. Thaddeus was the visionary behind the groundbreaking publication *Theology: A Portrait in Black* (1980). He collected and edited the papers, then published and circulated the manuscript. Because of Thaddeus, the legendary 'little green book' represents an important turning point for black Catholic scholarship. Because of his influence on Black Catholic life, teaching, and scholarship, he arguably joins the ranks of Daniel Rudd (1854-1933), journalist and founder of the first National Black Catholic Congress, and Dr. Thomas Wyatt Turner (1877-1978), founder of the Federated Colored Catholics (FCC).

Thaddeus is remembered fondly by former students, university colleagues, and members of the BCTS.[6] His students remember him as a caring and attentive teacher. BCTS member Dr. Paul Green remembers his days at Cardinal Ritter: "Father taught me and so many other students at Cardinal Ritter College Preparatory High School in St. Louis, MO. He was far more to us than an educator. He reminded us that we have been and remain God's children. He made us feel and know that we could accomplish anything with God's love and God's grace." Former student Lisa von Feldt writes: "Thanks, Fr. Thad, for the words of

---

[6] Quotes from former students and colleagues are taken from the following two sources: "In Memoriam: Thaddeus Posey, O.F.M. Cap." BCTS – The Black Catholic Theological Symposium, last modified August 20, 2013, accessed September 10, 2013. http://www.bcts.org; and "Fr. Thaddeus Posey O.F.M. Cap.," *Denver Post Obituaries*, last modified August 10, 2013, accessed September 6, 2013, http://www.legacy.com/guestbooks/denverpost/guestbook.aspx?n=thaddeus-posey&pid=166348047#sthash.RHsrPQp2.dpbs.

wisdom in high school. You were an inspiration to a lot of kids, me included. Godspeed, teacher." BCTS member Claudine Pannell-Goodlett reflects on her time at the IBCS: "I was a student at the Institute when he was interim director. He provided invaluable guidance in pursuit of my studies of Black Catholic women."

Thaddeus also made an impression on his colleagues at the University of St. Thomas. Drs. Catherine Cory and Anne King reflect on their interactions with him. Dr. Cory writes: "Thanks to Fr. Thaddeus' community and family, we had the pleasure of having him as our colleague at the University of St. Thomas for more than a decade. He was passionate about the success of each of his students and always ready to listen when someone needed counsel. I miss his infectious smile and his welcoming presence. Thaddeus, may the angels lead you into paradise!" And Dr. King remembers his kindness and generosity: "Thaddeus was a wonderful person and colleague. I have missed him greatly since he moved out of Minnesota, although we emailed back and forth now and then. He gave me my only upgrade to first class travel on the way to a conference once – and we laughed a lot all the time."

BCTS members reflect on the significance of Thaddeus' contributions. Dr. Fr. Bryan Massingale writes: "Former director of the Institute for Black Catholic Studies, Thaddeus has had a pivotal influence on the shape of Black Catholicism in the United States." Dr. Shawn Copeland and Dr. Fr. Ed Branch comment on his heart and passion. Ed Branch writes: "An iconic member of the Clergy Caucus, he paid attention to what was happening to us personally and as an organization." Shawn Copeland reflects: "In all that Thaddeus did, he always had the Black Catholic community in mind and heart. If it were not for his energy and savvy and poise, the two 'institutions' in which many of us are so invested would not exist. He was/is truly committed to us for the glory of God and the good of the Church."

BCTS members Sr. Dr. Jamie Phelps and Fr. Dr. Charles Payne attended the wake and funeral for Fr. Thaddeus. Jamie Phelps writes of her impressions from the testimonials: "It became clear from the testimonies that Thaddeus embraced everyone from diverse cultural and racial backgrounds whom he met and deepened their consciousness of the cultural gifts with which African Americans have enriched our nation and church."

The BCTS remembers Fr. Thaddeus Posey for his dedication to social justice, not just for Black Catholics but for African Americans of every faith, and for all those who suffer from injustice and oppression. We remember him for his passion and honor him for his leadership. Whatever successes we may have today, we owe in large part to Fr. Thaddeus who fought for us throughout his entire career.

> Eternal rest, grant unto him O Lord
> and let perpetual light shine upon him.
>
> May he rest in peace. Amen.

Figure 9: Crest of the U.S. Army Chaplain Corps

Father Thaddeus Posey, O.F.M. Cap.

May 1944 ~ August 2013

WORKS CITED

BCTS. "In Memoriam: Thaddeus Posey, O.F.M. Cap." BCTS – The Black Catholic Theological Symposium. Last modified August 20, 2013. Accessed September 10, 2013. http://www.bcts.org.

Culver, Virginia. "People Watch Black Priest." *The Denver Post,* Friday December 21st, 1973.

Denver Post Obituaries. "Fr. Thaddeus Posey O.F.M. Cap." Accessed September 6, 2013. http://www.legacy.com/obituaries/denverpost/.

The Provincial Porter, A Newsletter of the Capuchin Province of Mid-America. Issue 139 (April 2007): 5. Accessed August 10, 2013. www.capuchins.org.

The Experience of the Oblate Sisters of Providence during the Civil War Era

Diane Batts Morrow
The University of Georgia

In this paper, based on a talk delivered during the 2012 Annual Meeting in Miami Gardens, Florida, Dr. Morrow delves into the annals of the Oblate Sisters of Providence and reveals the challenges they faced during the Civil War Era and their strength and ingenuity in finding resourceful solutions to continue in their mission to educate black children and provide much-needed services for slaves and free blacks during this time. Their capacity for commitment and creativity at this time of existential conflict stands as a model even today.

Black and free in a slave society that privileged only whiteness, female in a male dominated society, Roman Catholic in a Protestant society, and pursuing religious vocations in a society doubting the virtue of all black women, the Oblate Sisters of Providence proved exceptional in nineteenth-century America. Organized in 1828, the Oblate sisters dedicated themselves as "a Religious society of Coloured Women established in Baltimore with the [approval] of the Most Reverend Archbishop, [who] renounce the world to consecrate themselves to God, and to the Christian education of young girls of color."[1]

As did all communities of women religious, the Oblate sisterhood followed the ascetic lifestyle which their commitment to

---

[1] The Original Rule and Constitutions of the Oblate Sisters of Providence, English manuscript copy, RG III, Box 29, Folder 2, AOSP.

the vows of poverty, chastity, and obedience prescribed. However, the burden of the systemic racism pervading the slaveholding United States compounded the difficulties this black sisterhood had confronted during their existence of some thirty years. Oblate acceptance of adversity, however, did not require a passive resignation to white society's ascriptions of racial inferiority. Indeed, as they had from their origins, the sisters continued to defy such social derogation by defining themselves as women of virtue who exercised agency in service to others.

Oblate annals entries frequently documented the sisterhood's work in ministering to black Catholics. Not only did the reputation for excellence the Oblate school had earned over time attract pupils from beyond the immediate vicinity of Baltimore, but the sisters continued to serve as role models who attracted young women to religious life. During 1860 alone the Oblate community received five candidates as postulants, or entry level members, while six postulants received the religious habit, advancing to the rank of novice. The annals also noted regularly the sizeable attendance of black Catholics at religious ceremonies in the Oblate St. Frances Chapel.

In addition to meeting the spiritual needs of black Catholics, the sisters addressed their physical needs as well. In April, 1860 the Oblate community opened a Widows and Aged People's Home. This act merely formalized a service the sisters had been providing since their first decade of existence, when they had stipulated the financial and lifestyle conditions under which elderly women could reside in the Oblate convent, thus providing a welcome alternative to the city poorhouse attic accommodations for elderly women of color. Since their establishment the Oblate sisterhood had also housed and educated a number of orphan girls, whom they referred to as "children of the house." While several of these girls later found employment outside the convent, others joined the Oblate sisterhood.[2]

On 4 November, the annals entry stated, "On this day we received the sad although not unexpected news that our worthy and kind Director was to leave us and that our beloved Church was to be closed. It is impossible to describe our feelings at such an event...it was truly a mournful occasion." On 5 November, the annalist pointedly observed, "It was remarkable that it was the anniversary of the death of our beloved Founder that this sudden change took place."[3] For the sizable Oblate membership old enough to have experienced the wrenching communal crises following the death in 1843 of their co-founder and first spiritual director, the Sulpician priest James Hector Joubert, the simultaneous departure of their current Redemptorist director, Fr. Dominic Kraus, and closing of their chapel as a public church could only have reawakened difficult and painful memories of clerical abandonment.[4]

However, the sequence of events over the next several days surely relieved any Oblate concerns. On 7 November Oblate Superior Gertrude Thomas accompanied by one of the sisters visited the Superior of the Jesuits now charged with Oblate spiritual direction. He received his visitors kindly and promised to do whatever lay in his power for the good of the community. He appointed Rev. Peter Miller as Oblate spiritual director. On 10 November the annalist reported, "We had Mass today for the first time by our new Director. He has very kindly allotted twelve pews in Blessed Peter Claver Chapel for the use of the [Sisters] and Children."[5]

---

[2] Morrow, *Persons of Color*, 103, 107, 161.
[3] Oblate Annals, 4, 5 November 1860, RG II, Box 34, Folder 4, AOSP.
[4] See Morrow, *Persons of Color*, chapter 8.
[5] Oblate Annals, 7, 10 November 1860, RG II, Box 34, Folder 4, AOSP.

Oblate appreciation of Fr. Miller grew rapidly in the first months of his spiritual directorship. On 9 March 1861, "the feast of our holy mother and patroness St. Frances," Miller celebrated Mass in the Oblate St. Frances Chapel "and afterwards gave a very moving and interesting discourse on the great virtues practiced by our glorious patroness. It was the first he had given and was on that account gratefully received and prized."[6] The following month, the course of history would impose unexpected changes throughout American society, including the Oblate Sisters of Providence.

The outbreak of the Civil War in April 1861 brought hardship and suffering to Americans in both the North and the South. The state of Maryland remained loyal to the Union, even as many of its slaveholding citizens identified with the Confederate cause. White Catholics—both nationally and in Maryland—expressed their hostility toward black people as emphatically as did their Protestant fellow citizens. The pages of the *Catholic Mirror*, the official publication of the archdiocese of Baltimore, amply documented these white sentiments.

A week and a day after the commencement of hostilities, the *Mirror*'s editorial, "The War," vigorously defended the institution of slavery. It warned New Englanders against "the very common mistake of putting self in the place of the slave and imagining what a terrible infliction it would be." For white men, "it were indeed worse than death." These northerners, however, "...quite forget that the slave has been born to his lot, as were his fathers before him and that he feels in it neither degradation nor misery. He is practically better off than the majority of laborers anywhere in the civilized world….He is at home a singularly happy and contented man. He never works so hard during the day but that he is ready to

---

[6] Ibid., 9 March 1861, RG II, Box 34, Folder 5, AOSP.

sing, dance, and play the fiddle nearly all night....."[7] Such assertions pervaded the pages of the *Catholic Mirror* and other Maryland publications throughout the war. Not only do they provide transfixing insights into the racial convictions of the majority of white Marylanders, they also elucidate the social climate in which black people in general and the Oblate Sisters in particular functioned during this time.

Baltimoreans seldom witnessed actual military combat within the city, but the war still affected their daily lives. Significantly, the Oblate Annals did not mention the tumult of war that April. The Oblate Sisters followed their community life and conducted their schools as closely as possible according to their accustomed patterns, but war conditions inevitably disrupted the normal course of Oblate life, as the annalist's occasional references to the events of the war revealed.

The sisters' response to their first encounter with adverse Civil War conditions demonstrated characteristic Oblate initiative and resourcefulness. On 26 December 1861, the annalist noted, "Owing to the difficulty of receiving payment from the parents of the children, as all Communication is stopped, it was judged advisable by our friends to have a Concert for the benefit of the school." The first concert occurred the day after Christmas, attracted a large audience and netted $100 in revenue.[8] Fund raising concerts, a necessary response which wartime conditions generated, became a staple resource in the Oblate arsenal to maintain financial solvency.

On 10 April 1862 the annalist reported that boarding pupil Brittannia Ferguson from Richmond, Virginia—the capital of the Confederacy—had battled a serious illness for several months. She died on Sunday, 20 April. On Tuesday 22 April the annalist

---

[7] "The War," *Catholic Mirror*, 20 April 1861, XII, # 16, p. 4.
[8] Oblate Annals, 26 December 1861, RG II, Box 34, Folder 5, AOSP.

reported, "Brittannia was buried today. Rev. Father Miller sang a Requiem Mass, after which she was put in a vault until some news from her home." This last information constituted an indirect reference to the intrusion of war. Undoubtedly the same cessation of communication and tuition payments associated with the war the previous year prevented reliable communications with the Ferguson family about Brittannia's condition and final disposition.[9]

Occasionally conditions the Civil War created proved positive for the Oblate community. On Sunday, 7 September the annalist stated, "Through the kindness of our good father we had Mass today in our Chapel as on account of the Railroad being destroyed several of the fathers could not get to Frederick." The next day the sisters enjoyed three Masses and Holy Communion "for the same reason above mentioned." The sisters again held a concert to raise funds for the school the day after Christmas. From 22 December through New Year's Day, the sisters also held a fund raising sale which "closed on New Year's day with a general raffle. The Proceeds of the Whole amounted to $250.00."[10]

On 24 May 1863 a benefit concert netted $84.00. The annalist continued, "We intended to repeat the Concert, but owing to the disturbed state of the City as Martial law was declared we were obliged to postpone it until some time later." The next entry, dated 20 July noted briefly, "Our schools closed today, we had no Exhibition for the reason mentioned above."[11] When the military authorities declared martial law, people could not travel freely on the streets, especially after dark. This 1863 concert postponement and cancellation of their annual school closing ceremonies constituted the most direct Civil War intrusions on Oblate activities.

---

[9] Ibid., 10, 20, 22, April 1862.
[10] Ibid., 7, 8 September, 26 December, 1862.
[11] Ibid., 14 January, 9 March, 24 May, 20 July 1863.

However, the Oblate community also realized their long cherished goal to establish schools for black children beyond the city of Baltimore for the first time in the year 1863. Since 1833 the Oblate Sisters had expressed their missionary zeal and determined dedication "to God in the religious state to work more efficaciously for their sanctification and to contribute all the means in their power for the glory of God and the religious education of the girls of their race." Therefore they "at all times" stood "ready to go anywhere" that their clerical superiors "should judge the Holy Will of God called them."[12] Clerical timidity or indifference toward educating black children rather than Oblate commitment explained the thirty year interval before Oblate evangelical fervor acquired a promising field of labor.

On 4 August the annalist recorded, "Our Rev. father director today received an application from Rev. father Barbelin to establish a branch of our Community in Philadelphia. [I]t was a most unexpected proposal which everyone wished might be successful." From receipt of the initial inquiry to the proposed opening of the school in Philadelphia on the last Monday in August, the Oblate sisterhood allotted only three weeks, demonstrating the sincerity of their pledge to stand "at all times" "ready to go anywhere" to fulfill their teaching mission.

On 26 August the annalist recorded, "The Sisters started today for their new home. Our Rev. Director and Mother went on. It was a very sad parting as it was the first time some of them had left dear St. Frances. We who remained felt quite lost for some days, but happily being very busy we had no time to think."[13] Perhaps the oldest Oblate Sisters who had experienced the communal rupture of the 1840s when three members departed from the

---

[12] Morrow, *Persons of Color*, 72. Quotations from Oblate Annals, Vol. 1, pp. 25, 33, RG II, Box 34, Folder 1, AOSP.

[13] Oblate Annals, 24, 25, 26 August, 1863, RG II, Box 34, Folder 5, AOSP.

order might have derived considerable comfort from the fact that the departure of three sisters from the motherhouse this time heralded an advancement of the Oblate vision.

On 9 April the Oblate community confronted a significant blow to their mission of education. The annalist reported, "About this time the Sisters' school at Federal Hill [St. Peter Claver] decreasing so much that the Sisters were unable to support themselves; it was decided after mature deliberation to close the school and the Srs. returned home."[14] The Civil War plausibly bore at least partial responsibility for the school's decline. Free black people functioned at the margins of Baltimore's economy and wartime conditions further eroded their employment opportunities, making it difficult for them to earn sufficient discretionary income to afford the modest tuition the Oblate schools charged.

According to its new constitution, the state of Maryland abolished slavery effective 1 November 1864. On 1 March 1865 the annalist reported," Our Reverend Director seeing the danger to which Catholic children are exposed of losing their faith, employed two of the Srs. to take charge of a Free school so that they might come and learn their religion and at the same time their learning would be attended to. This good father gave for these six months $75.00. The school numbers already 60 scholars only girls."[15] Although unacknowledged here, contemporary developments in Maryland society plausibly prompted Miller's unprecedented generosity in personally subsidizing a free black school at this particular time. Historian Paul Fuke argues persuasively that during this period in Maryland black people seized the initiative in providing both educational opportunities and social services for

---

[14] Ibid., 9April 1864.
[15] Ibid., 1 March 1865.

their own race.[16] In significant ways Oblate educational initiatives resonated with this black community drive. Perhaps Miller and the Oblate Sisters specifically thought of the needs of the newly freed but poor people in opening this free school a few months later. Former pupils of the Oblate St. Peter Claver School, closed the previous year, might also attend this free school.

Just as the Oblate annals did not note the beginning of the Civil War in April 1861, they did not mention the end of hostilities in April 1865. The only annals entry for the month of April that year remarked, "We had the happiness of having a low Mass today in our Chapel so that the Srs. might make their Easter [duty]...," as befitted the concerns of a community of women religious.[17]

The Civil War had imposed unanticipated obstacles on the routine of Oblate life, ranging from the disruption of lines of communication to the imposition of martial law. In correspondence with a Freedmen's Bureau official in 1867 the sisterhood disclosed, referring to themselves in the third person, "During the war they clothed, fed, and furnished with books 8 children from Southern States, whose Parents were unable to transmit funds, and since the

---

[16] Richard Paul Fuke, *Imperfect Equality: African Americans and the Confines of White Racial Attitudes in Post-Emancipation Maryland* (New York: Fordham University Press, 1999), 88. In addition to this source, for insightful and detailed treatments of both black agency in effecting freedom and the obstacles black people encountered in the process see Fields, Barbara J. *Slavery and Freedom on the Middle Ground: Maryland During the Nineteenth Century* (New Haven: Yale University Press, 1985). For excellent primary source collections documenting the black experience during the Civil War era, see C. Peter Ripley et al, editors, *Witness for Freedom: African American Voices on Race, Slavery, and Emancipation*(Chapel Hill: The University of North Carolina Press, 1993); Ira Berlin et al, editors, *Free at Last: A Documentary History of Slavery, Freedom, and the Civil War* (New York: The New Press, 1992); and Ira Berlin et al, editors, *Freedom: A Documentary History of Emancipation, 1861-1867* Series I, Vol.II, The Wartime Genesis of Free Labor: The Upper South (Cambridge and New York: Cambridge University Press, 1993).

[17] Oblate Annals, 13 April 1865, RG II, Box 34, Folder 5, AOSP.

close of the War they have been unsuccessful in receiving pay."[18] Nevertheless, the sisters responded to these difficulties with resourcefulness, instituting fund raising concerts to augment dwindling tuition payments. Furthermore, under adverse wartime conditions the sisters succeeded in advancing their education mission on two separate fronts. They opened their first Oblate colony outside Baltimore in Philadelphia in 1863 and a free school in Baltimore in 1865 to accommodate pupils from both the financially constrained antebellum free and the newly emancipated but impoverished black populations. Not only had the Oblate Sisters of Providence survived the Civil War as a viable and functioning community of black women religious educators, but they also stood poised at the dawn of the Reconstruction era to expand the services they offered to their people as they encountered the realities of freedom in postwar American society.

* * *

April, 1865 through early 1867, the era of Presidential Reconstruction following the Civil War, boded ill for most black people in the United States. Presidents Lincoln and Johnson adopted policies to restore the sundered Union as quickly and painlessly as possible by imposing minimal demands on the former Confederacy to effect political reunion, property restoration—with the notable exception of human property—and minimal federal intrusion in the conduct of state affairs. The welfare of black people proved of low priority to these administrations. In Maryland the former slaveholding elite soon enforced Black Codes and manipulated apprenticeship laws to remove black children from

---

[18] Oblate Sisters of Providence to William Howard Day, Esq., Superintendent of Freedmen's Schools, 22 October 1867, Records of the field offices for the states of Maryland and Delaware, Bureau of Refugees, Freedmen, and Abandoned Lands, 1865-1892, RG 105, Microfilm Roll # 4, Target 1: Office of the Assistant Commissioner Correspondence, Unregistered Letters Received, October 1865 - November 1868.

their parents, which threatened to eviscerate any substance from the meaning of freedom for black people.

An informative depiction of continuing negative white Catholic feeling toward black people appeared in the *Catholic Mirror* editorial, "The Future of the Negro," in the 2 December 1865 issue. The author asserted, "If the negro race can be elevated in the scale of being, we look to the ministers of the Catholic religion to solve the problem and achieve the good work." He further lamented, "But slavery which did so much to civilize the race is among the dead fossils of the past, and the negro is thrown upon his own resources to decide the question of his capacity for self-government. We know that he is unfitted by habits, education, or a previous appreciation of the civilizing arts of freedom, to discharge the duties of the citizen, or to lift the slave into the intelligent member of society." Insisting that "The Catholic Church can soften the rudeness of his heart, and elevate him to a standard of comparative equality with the white race—Nature has not made him *even in possibility*, the equal of the white man [emphasis his]...," the author concluded, "hence if he ever reach that comparative equality..., we maintain that the Catholic Church alone can qualify him...."[19] Neither in their blanket dismissal of black capabilities "to lift the slave into the intelligent member of society" nor in their conviction of the Catholic Church's mandate to regenerate the black race did the editors once consider the seminal mission of the Oblate Sisters of Providence.

Even during this difficult period black individuals and groups continued to exert agency to improve conditions for themselves and others. Contemporary white witnesses documented the substantial accomplishments of black people, particularly in the field of education. The 1866 report of a white organization

---

[19] "The Future of the Negro," *Catholic Mirror*, XVI, # 48, 2 December 1865, p. 4.

observed, "But most of all we have been cheered by the eagerness to learn manifested by the Colored People, and by their willingness to contribute toward the payment of the expense of their own education." Of $27,800 "total amount of certain receipts" for the coming year, black people in Baltimore and the counties had provided $11,800.[20]

Oblate annals entries during the summer months following the end of the war heralded several first experiences for the sisterhood. On 7 August the annalist referred to the original St. Frances School for Colored Girls founded in 1828 as the Academy for the first time. The recent establishment of the Oblate free school probably encouraged this new characterization. Starting in 1867 Fr. Miller and several of his Jesuit colleagues associated with Loyola College would upgrade the Oblate school's curriculum to effect substantive as well as this nominal change.

The annalist continued, "Through the kindness of our good father he sent for two girls who formerly belonged to them, one he will send to Phila[delphia] so that she may attend to the house work and at the same time the Srs. will teach her and the other will remain with us."[21] As stated earlier, the Oblate annals rarely referred to worldly affairs such as slavery and the Civil War explicitly. Throughout the antebellum period virtually all of the white sisterhoods and orders of priests in the archdiocese of Baltimore had participated in and profited from the institution of slavery. The formerly enslaved status of several of its members proved the only association connecting the Oblate sisterhood to slavery.[22] Nevertheless, this simple statement that the Oblate

---

[20] *Second Annual Report of the Baltimore Association for the Moral and Educational Improvement of the Colored People* (Baltimore: J. B. Rose &,Co., November, 1866), 4, 8, 4-5.

[21] Ibid., 7 August 1865.

[22] For an analysis of the Catholic Church's position on slavery see Morrow, *Persons of Color*, 79, 116-17, 250-51, 256-57, 68-70, 211-12.

community would absorb and educate two women the Jesuit priests had formerly owned constituted another example of Oblate commitment to assist their people in the challenging transition from slavery to freedom.

New candidates continued to increase the membership of the Oblate community during 1866. Julia Brown arrived from St. Louis on 15 May "well recommended by...the Srs. of Mercy." From Washington, D.C., Sally Adams entered the sisterhood on 26 July "highly recommended by...the Sisters of Charity with whom she has been living." Oblate annals did not specify the nature of the relationship between either Brown and the Sisters of Mercy or Adams and the Sisters of Charity which informed their respective recommendations of these candidates' suitability for religious life. As religious orders had owned slaves in both St. Louis and the nation's capital, these sisterhoods plausibly might have recommended their former property for Oblate membership.[23]

On 30 August the annalist mentioned for the first time a signal event which directed the Oblate sisterhood on a new mission trajectory. She stated, "About this time preparations were begun to open the Orphan Asylum that our good father [Miller] had for some time been seriously thinking on." While Miller had conceived the idea of the orphan asylum, early on in the process he had sought and gained the cooperation of the Oblate Sisters to staff it.

The severe dislocation and rupture of black families which the war, emancipation, and subsequent significant migration of the formerly enslaved, rural black people to urban centers like Baltimore had occasioned certainly warranted the necessity of the orphan asylum. As they had in establishing schools, black people seized the initiative in providing social services for their own, but available black resources remained insufficient to meet the

---

[23] Oblate Annals, 15 May, 26 July 1866, RG II, Box 34, Folder 5, AOSP.

daunting need. Fuke explained, "Clearly black Baltimoreans did the best they could under difficult circumstances. Equally clearly, they did so without a lot of help from the white community. Indeed, whites tended in the end to consign responsibility for social problems to those most affected by them—blacks themselves." Significantly, in this discussion of black agency Fuke featured the Oblate Sisters' orphan asylum as an iconic example of black self-help.[24]

On 7 October 1866 the Second Plenary Council convened in Baltimore for two weeks with much pomp and circumstance. The daily parade of visiting prelates and dignitaries proved especially significant for the Oblate community on 7 October when Archbishop Jean-Marie Odin of New Orleans visited them to request an Oblate mission in his city. Miller specified that Odin "should pay the Srs. passage and have a house ready for them. He said that as soon as he arrived home he would attend to it."[25] The three assigned sisters departed for New Orleans on 9 February 1867.

The following month Odin penned a very interesting and revealing letter to his friend, Archbishop Spalding of Baltimore, concerning the Oblate Sisters. He reported, "Our Oblate Sisters arrived in good health....Our colored population as well as the white people appeared pleased with the introduction of the sisters in our city. They will have, I am sure, a vast field for usefulness. We have already eight or ten schools for the Africans which succeed well. Several of our white teachers have overcome the prejudices of the country and devote themselves to the instruction of the colored race. Their efforts are pleasing to the community which

---

[24] Fuke, *Imperfect Equality*, 126-27.
[25] Ibid., 7 October 1866.

feels the necessity of retaining that class of people in the country for field and housework."[26]

Even as Odin assured Spalding of the Oblate Sisters' safe arrival and welcome to New Orleans, he revealed the limiting parameters within which he—and by extension white society in general—expected them to exercise their "usefulness." His reference to the freed people as "Africans" expressed the alienation and foreignness with which much of white society still regarded black people, who had resided in this country for centuries, frequently on the most intimate of terms with its white citizenry. The arrival of the Oblate Sisters may have pleased the white and black populations of New Orleans for diametrically opposed reasons. Black people may have envisioned an Oblate education as providing essential tools toward realizing the potential of emancipation, culminating in full participation in American society. White people—including those several teachers of the colored race Odin cited above—may have interpreted their role as contributing to controlling "that class of people" which necessity compelled them to retain "in the country for field and housework," that is, to serve white society's needs as they had under enslavement, not to enjoy the fruits of inclusion in the American polity. In significant ways Odin's letter echoed the duality regarding black people plaguing not only the Catholic Church in the United States but also much of white American society: they considered black people in, but not of, both Church and society and capable at most of a "comparative equality" with the white race, the parameters of which white people intended to define exclusively.

---

[26] 36A Q6, Jean-Marie, Archbishop of New Orleans to Most Rev. Dear Sir, 1 March 1867, AAB, AASMSU.

The years 1867-1877 formed the era in United States history known as radical or Congressional Reconstruction, a period when the federal government for a time acted more assertively in formulating policies and establishing institutions to safeguard the interests of the recently emancipated black people. A reinvigorated Bureau of Refugees, Abandoned Lands, and Freedmen—or Freedmen's Bureau—constituted a widely recognized and reviled iteration of federal intervention in the South. Although Bureau involvement in labor contracts, the administration of justice, land disbursements, and relief allocations proved controversial, its efforts in the field of education remained its signal and most enduring success.[27] The Oblate Sisters of Providence shared with the Freedmen's Bureau an interest in the education of black people.

The 1867 Oblate schools closing exercises precipitated an extraordinary sequence of events. The Moses Lake family of Annapolis had actively participated in the informal lay black Catholic support network of the Oblate Sisters since the 1840s and they demonstrated their continuing devotion to the Oblate mission by inviting a special guest to the sisters' 1867 closing exercises. What he witnessed on that occasion so impressed the noted black publisher, educator, and racial spokesman, William Howard Day, that he wrote an article about it the following September. Day

---

[27] For thorough discussions of the Freedmen's Bureau and education see, among others, Eric Foner, *Reconstruction: America's Unfinished Revolution* (New York: Harper and Row,1988); Leon Litwack, *Been in the Storm So Long: The Aftermath of Slavery* (New York: Random House, 1979); James D. Anderson, *The Education of Blacks in the South, 1860-1935* (Chapel Hill: The University of North Carolina Press, 1988); Ronald Butchart, *Northern Schools, Southern Blacks, and Reconstruction: Freedmen's Education, 1862-1875* (Westport, CN: Praeger, 1980); Jacqueline Jones, *Soldiers of Light and Love: Northern Teachers and Georgia Blacks, 1865–1873* (Chapel Hill: The University of North Carolina Press, 1980).

served as Superintendent of Schools for the Freedmen in Maryland and Delaware for the Freedmen's Bureau in 1867-68.[28]

Day pronounced himself "exceedingly gratified with the appearance of the various Departments and the ability and urbanity of the Teachers." While averring, "Being a Protestant, we could not be expected to endorse all the views held and taught in the Academy;" Day nevertheless avowed, "but we feel that it is due to the energy, efficiency, and thoroughness exhibited in the Departments visited to say that we wish our Protestant friends had Church Schools half so good." Day concluded, "Only those who have lived in Maryland during the dark days of Bondage can fully realize of how much service this School has been…. While white schools (so called) shut out colored young ladies, this and other similar schools under the control of the Catholic portion of community opened their doors and threw around the colored girls that protection which others denied. It is not strange therefore, that colored young ladies of excellent families have flocked to this and similar institutions….The sisters of Providence have set a noble example which it would be suicidal in Protestants not to follow."[29]

As impelled by their dire financial straits as encouraged by Day's highly favorable review of their efforts, the Oblate Sisters wrote an extraordinary letter to Superintendent of Freedmen's Schools Day in October. This letter remains particularly informative as one of the few extant expressions of how the Oblate Sisters interpreted their historic mission and current active role in ministering to the freed people to persuade a federal bureaucracy

---

[28] For a thorough discussion of Day's life and significant accomplishments, see R. J Blackett, "Marching On: The Life of William Howard Day," chap. In *Beating Against the Barriers: The Lives of Six Nineteenth-Century Afro-Americans* (Ithaca and London: Cornell University Press, 1989), 286-386.

[29] "The St. Frances Academy," *Zion's Standard and Weekly Review*, 4 September 1867 [newspaper title identified in Oblate correspondence to Day cited below], Vertical File 446, AOSP.

of the legitimacy of their unprecedented request for governmental assistance.

The introductory sentence stated their purpose succinctly by explaining, "The very flattering notice in the *Zion's Standard and Weekly Review* of September 4, 1867 of our Academy, and the zeal you have shown in the moral and intellectual education of the children of our race lead us to hope that the reports herein enclosed will be favorably received by you, and that you will by your influence endeavor to obtain from the Freedmen's Bureau some pecuniary aid to enable us to continue the good work in which you yourself are so deeply interested." The sisters emphasized the non-denominational nature of their ministry, stating that "During the 38 years of the existence of our schools the number of Pupils was at least 1500 scholars of whom 800 at least were of a different denomination from that of the Sisters."[30]

The description of the Oblate free school, begun in 1865 "to further the advancement of our race and rescue many children from ignorance," stated that the school enrolled 50 to 70 pupils annually and incurred among other expenses the $1500 purchase price of its building. The following year the orphan asylum opened "to rescue from want and misery many young children left helpless by the ravages of war or poverty" and received female orphans of all religious denominations from infancy to sixteen years of age. It currently housed 25 inmates and purchasing and furnishing the orphanage had cost the community $3300. The letter specifically noted, "We have depended upon the charitable collections of the

---

[30] Oblate Sisters of Providence to William Howard Day, Esq., Superintendent of Freedmen's Schools, 22 October 1867, Records of the field offices for the states of Maryland and Delaware, Bureau of Refugees, Freedmen, and Abandoned Lands, 1865-1892, RG 105, Microfilm Roll # 4, Target 1: Office of the Assistant Commissioner Correspondence, Unregistered Letters Received, October 1865 - November 1868.

Colored people for the maintenance and clothing of the orphans."[31]

Assuring Superintendent Day that "the Sisters have never received one dollar of assistance from the State or General Government," they nevertheless reasoned "that the Free School and Orphan Asylum seem to fall under the class of schools which since the war the General Government has so nobly maintained in this and other States." The letter further revealed, "The teachers in the Free School and Orphan Asylum receive no pay for their services, being supported by the labor of their hands by sewing, etc and by the revenue from the Academy or Boarding School." The letter then disclosed that "the debts of the various schools amount to $8000 and the income from the Academy is only about $4000, leaving us struggling for the maintenance of the Free School and Orphan Asylum." In a final plea for Day's intercession on their behalf, the sisters stated directly, "The continuance of the Free School and Orphan Asylum must depend upon the very precarious collections from our poor race, unless your influence and charity shall come to our assistance by obtaining for us some substantial recognition from the General Government."[32]

Although four days after receiving their correspondence, Day dutifully referred this Oblate manifesto to his superior, Major General E. M. Gregory, assistant commissioner of the Freedmen's Bureau, the sisters received nothing from the Bureau. They did, however, continue to maintain their charitable institutions with the income they derived from their own labors, academy tuitions and fees, and the "very precarious collections from our poor race."

For the remainder of the Reconstruction era the Oblate Sisters confronted and surmounted several challenges. In 1870 they

---

[31] Ibid.
[32] Ibid.

learned the unexpected news that the city of Baltimore planned to extend a street right through their property. After forty years of living on Richmond Street, the Sisters had to move to a new home. The city paid the Sisters enough money for them to begin but not to complete construction of a new residence on Chase Street. The Oblates moved their convent, schools, and orphanage to Chase Street in 1871. St. Frances Academy remains at this same location today. Then, because of a lack of support, the Sisters reluctantly closed their schools in Philadelphia in 1871 and in New Orleans in 1873.

The Sisters, pupils, and orphans had appreciated Fr. Miller's love and concern for them over the years and they thanked God for His constant Providence toward them in the person of Fr. Miller. They worried, however, that Miller's constant exertions on behalf of the black community compromised his frail health. They had watched anxiously as he succumbed to the ravages of tuberculosis. Finally, on 26 September 1877, Fr. Peter Miller, S.J. died. Everyone in the St. Frances community cried out in grief and sorrow. The Sisters said, "We felt for the second time in the life of the community entire Orphans."[33] After Fr. Miller's death the Oblate Sisters encountered an uncertain future and new challenges.

The year 1877 proved critical for the United States as well. When Reconstruction ended that year, the Federal Government surrendered the black freedmen to the control of their former owners. The southern states worked to rebuild their world without slavery, but one which still separated black and white people as much as possible. As southern states passed laws to deny freedom and citizenship rights to the former slaves, the rest of the nation looked on in silence. The Oblate Sisters and their education mission

---

[33] Oblate Annals, 26 September 1877, RG II, Box 34, Folder 9, AOSP.

formed part of the solution black people developed on their own to confront the continuing challenges of freedom.

Diane Batts Morrow, Ph.D.

WORKS CITED

Primary Sources

Annals of the Oblate Sisters of Providence, RG II, Box 34, Folders 5-9, Archives of the Oblate Sisters of Providence, Baltimore, MD.

Catholic Mirror, 1861-65, Associated Archives at St. Mary's Seminary and University, Baltimore, MD.

First and Second Annual Reports of the Baltimore Association for the Moral and Educational Improvement of the Colored People. Baltimore: J. B. Rose & Co., 1865, 1866.

Original Rule and Constitutions of the Oblate Sisters of Providence, English manuscript copy, RG III, Box 29, Folder 2, AOSP.

Records of the field offices for the states of Maryland and Delaware, Bureau of Refugees, Freedmen, and Abandoned Lands, 1865-1892, RG 105, National Archives, Washington, D.C.

"The St. Frances Academy," *Zion's Standard and Weekly Review*, 4 September 1867, Vertical File 446, AOSP.

36A Q6, Jean-Marie, Archbishop of New Orleans to Most Rev. Dear Sir, 1 March 1867, Archives of the Archdiocese of Baltimore, Associated Archives at St. Mary's Seminary and University, Baltimore, MD.

Secondary Sources

Fuke, Paul R. *Imperfect Equality: African Americans and the Confines of White Racial Attitudes in Post-Emancipation Maryland.* New York: Fordham University Press, 1999.

Morrow, Diane Batts. *Persons of Color and Religious at the Same Time: The Oblate Sisters of Providence, 1828-1860.* Chapel Hill: The University of North Carolina Press, 2002.

Suffering As Glory In Hans Urs Von Balthasar And James Cone

Joseph Flipper
Bellarmine University

Katy Leamy
Mount Angel Seminary

Based on the paper they delivered during the 2012 Annual Meeting, Flipper and Leamy elaborate the implications of the respective reflections on the crucifixion of Christ and his descent into hell in the work of Hans Urs von Balthasar and James H. Cone. They conclude that, together, Balthasar and Cone supply a theological justification for seeing the oppressed and rejected as the privileged media of God's glorious revelation.

Frederick Flemister (1917-1976) captured a synoptic understanding of the cross and lynching in his painting *The Mourners* (ca. 1940).[1] In *The Mourners*, a black man stripped of his clothes lies on the ground, surrounded by people in mourning. The man's head and upper body are supported by a woman in a representation of Michelangelo's Pietà. A tree with a rope dangling from the branch is in the foreground. In the background stand vague silhouettes of riders on horseback, presumably silhouettes of the murderers. A female figure at the center of the painting lifts both arms to the sky, in a posture reflective of mourning or praise. A striking feature of the painting is its lack of partition between the religious subject and the secular. It is unclear whether it is a

---

[1] Stacy I. Morgan, *Rethinking Social Realism: African American Art and Literature, 1930-1953* (Athens, GA: University of Georgia Press, 2004), 146.

depiction of lynching with religious allusions or a depiction of Christ with allusions to lynching. Moreover, it is indeterminate whether this death is a tragedy or a victory, or both.

The same indeterminacy and lack of partition marks the reflections of Swiss theologian Hans Urs von Balthasar (1905-1988) and James H. Cone (1938-pressent?) on the death of Christ. Both Balthasar and Cone follow the Gospel of John insofar as they present a paradoxical vision of Christ who is simultaneously abandoned on the cross and glorified by the Father.[2] Both Balthasar and Cone have embraced the Johannine identification of suffering with glory in Christ and its implications for human beings by envisioning the bodies of the abandoned, rejected, and murdered as the sites of God's glorious revelation.

We argue that Balthasar and Cone supply a needed eschatological optic for the transformation of suffering and the redemption of inescapable evil. First, Balthasar's theology of Christ's descent into hell articulates a vision of Christ's glorification as his total solidarity with human beings who experience the isolation of hell. Second, Cone's recent work *The Cross and the*

---

[2] The Gospel of John presents a paradoxical vision of Jesus' identity. Jesus simultaneously shares in the glory of the Father before the foundation of the world, and is abandoned, cursed, and dying on a cross. In him we see the Father's judgment upon the world and God's love for the world—even sinners. The gospel narrative shifts between perspective of glorification and suffering, always pointing ahead to the hour in which the fullness of glory will be revealed, when Jesus will be lifted up and his identity as Son of Man will be clarified. The clarification however, plunges us into a much deeper mystery: It is on the cross that the glory of God is revealed, and "the Way to the Father" opened for humanity. In the Johannine vision, the cross is not a mere gateway to glory. Nor is Jesus' suffering a cosmic payoff to the Father that gets humanity out of trouble. It is the absolute obedient self-abandonment itself that constitutes glory and life. This Johannine theology of the cross presents a strange and challenging optic in which the glory of God is revealed in abandonment, rejection, and suffering. By extension, the human share in this glorious life can be found in suffering abandonment, rejection, and even death.

Lynching Tree (2011), drawing from the religious imagination of the black church, argues that the lynched body existentially participates in the cross of Christ. We argue that Cone and Balthasar's shared ethical and theological insight lends a Christological meaning to the inescapable reality of suffering experienced by human beings and suggests the lynched body as the privileged place for encountering God's glorious revelation.[3]

II. Christ in Hell: Balthasar's Theology of the Descent

Balthasar first published *Mysterium Paschale: The Mystery of Easter* in 1970 under the German title *Theologie der Drie Tage* [*Theology of the Three Days*] as a theological meditation on the three days that Jesus spent in the grave.[4] Provocatively, Balthasar argued against a longstanding theological assumption about those three days. It had become conventional to think that the suffering of Christ ended with his death. In this account, Christ victoriously descended to Sheol, the realm of the Old Testament saints, to free them from death. In contrast, Balthasar posited that Christ descended into the experience of hell itself in the form of total abandonment by God. Taking literally the axiom "what is not assumed is not saved," Balthasar argues that Jesus assumed the existential condition of a humanity entirely cut off from relation with God. However, because he assumes this rejection of relation or depersonalization as God's absolute "yes" to relation, Jesus

---

[3] Christopher Pramuk develops a similar eschatological reflection on suffering and revelation. He approaches the topic of suffering from the lens of the communion with the dead, indicating that the "dangerous memory of Black suffering function[s] somehow as a source of White revelation." Christopher Pramuk, "'Strange Fruit': Black Suffering/White Revelation," *Theological Studies* 67 (2006): 347. While Pramuk elaborates a process of conversion of whites resulting in revelation, we seek to elaborate how Christ's solidarity with the dead makes the victim of oppression and violence the privileged medium of God's revelation.
[4] Hans Urs Von Balthasar, *Mysterium Paschale: The Mystery of Easter* (San Francisco: Ignatius Press, 2000).

opens the rejection, isolation, and abandonment of hell to the possibility of relation, to the glory of God.

How is it possible that God's glory is revealed in Christ's suffering on the cross and descent into hell? Balthasar takes seriously the notion that Jesus is God's Word about himself, the clearest articulation of divine glory. As a result, Jesus' experience—the suffering, death, and descent into hell—expresses this glory just as much as the concepts of divine blessedness and power. In fact, Christ's powerlessness in the grave is the definitive revelation of divine power, glory, and the blessedness of the Triune life. So, how does Balthasar deal with the apparent contradiction between the suffering experienced in powerlessness and death and the glory of God's almighty power and the blessedness of heaven?

We must briefly delve into Balthasar's Trinitarian theology to show how Balthasar holds these concepts together. Put simply, the glory of heaven consists in the eternal self-giving of the Divine persons in relation. Divine personhood, in a sense, is constituted by the eternal *kenosis* (self-emptying) that takes place between the Father and the Son and the Holy Spirit. This claim avoids a false distinction between God's essence and the persons of the Trinity.[5] God's essence *is* the divine relations, that is, what the divine persons do. The scriptures give us the key.

---

[5] We cannot become trapped in a false distinction between God's essence and the Divine Persons, where essence seems to be an impersonal set of properties such as immutability and omnipotence rather than relation. Within this paradigm the glory of the Divine essence would in fact preclude the possibility of god-abandonedness constituting the Divine Persons. Instead, Balthasar claims that the divine essence is precisely the relation between the persons. Christ's death on the cross and descent into hell is not just an economic aberration in the divine life, but rather a window into the eternal relation between the divine persons that is the life of God.

Glory and Kenosis

The Philippians Christ Hymn states that the Son emptied himself, taking the form of a slave (Phil. 2:7). This self-emptying—*kenosis*—in becoming human is the revelation of an eternal Triune *kenosis*.[6] Self-emptying love *is* who God is eternally. Christ's emptying of himself on the cross is thus the revelation of the eternal glory, a revelation expressed fully in the cross and the descent to hell. To put it bluntly, Balthasar is saying that the suffering, god-abandoned man who dies on a tree reveals the eternal Triune life of God. If this is true, then our previous concepts of the life, freedom, and power of God must be nailed to the cross. Our understanding of the essence of God or divine properties like immutability and omnipotence must be nailed to the cross. Now, the cross is the only place to find God.

A difficult paradox arises from Balthasar's Trinitarian theology. The life of God entails such an absolute self-offering as to be a kind of death. God's freedom entails loving obedience. God's power is the capacity to say "thy will, not mine" rather than "my will, not thine." The very same surrender of Christ to death is the power that conquers sin and death. As a result, the cross reveals God's glory; God's glory shines in the broken body given to us. The cross also reveals humanity's path to sharing in the glory of God. Balthasar's reflection on the cross is not novel. It draws from the

---

[6] It is important to note here that Balthasar's Trinitarian theology does not imply that the creaturely suffering that Christ undergoes somehow constitutes divine suffering or completes the divine kenosis. Rather Christ's suffering and descent into hell reveal an eternal immanent Triune reality. The eternal relation of blessedness that constitutes the Divine persons is a dynamic relation of self-emptying love. Each Person is an act of self-offering to the others. This concept—Divine personhood as an eternal relation of kenotic love—allows Balthasar to say that the immutable glory of God is revealed in the cry of a man who does not come down from the cross, "My God, why have you abandoned me?" (Mt. 27:46).

Gospel of John in which Jesus announces both the glorification of the Son (being "lifted up") and the suffering of the Messiah. John culminates in a scandalous conclusion: through the lens of God's love, glory and suffering are one and the same.

Balthasar's theological reflection moves from Holy Friday to Holy Saturday, from a meditation on the cross to a meditation on the descent to the grave. Balthasar's understanding of Christ's descent is shaped by two interrelated reflections: first, hell is, in essence, the loss of communion taken to its logical conclusion; second, the solidarity of Christ with humanity requires that he experiences this loss of communion.

Christ in Hell

Martin Luther, following Augustine, characterizes the sinful soul as *incurvatus in se*, curved in on itself.[7] We might say a self entirely consumed by self-absorption. For Balthasar, sin makes one "curved upon oneself" precisely by cutting off the relationships that make one a "person." Hell, in effect, is the sacrament of sin. It is the total absence of communion made real through death, impossible to escape. A cinematic version of this idea was presented in *What Dreams May Come* (1998), in which the character played by Robin Williams searches for his wife in the afterlife. In mourning for her husband, she commits suicide. Her experience of hell is the endless cycle of self-blame and suicide. There is nothing but the self to blame and nothing but the self to experience.

What Dreams May Come captures something of Balthasar's understanding of hell. According to Balthasar, hell or Sheol is not a mere external punishment for doing evil, as portrayed by

---

[7] Matt Jenson, *The Gravity of Sin: Augustine, Luther, and Barth on 'Homo Incurvatus in Se'* (New York: T & T Clark, 2006).

imaginative depictions of the fires of hell or demons, but instead is the inner experience and total orientation of the person. Hell is not a juridical result, but rather the natural consequence of evil. The effect bears the virtual impression of the cause, just as the brand is the virtual impression of the hot iron. Evil is the sacrament of hell, for it both signifies and brings about the mystery of iniquity in the very heart of the person. Hell is absolute self-possession that results in the absence of the possibility of relationship with the other, or any other. It is the erasure of the "likeness to God," the openness to relation and the possibility of love. In Balthasar's striking account, hell becomes the common experience of the sinner as well as those sinned against. The perpetrator of evil and the victim are both caught in evil's inescapable logic by which the possibility of communion with the other is dissolved.[8] The possibility of communion and, therefore, personhood, is eroded in this state.

Balthasar contends that the reality of the cross assumes that Christ experiences not just the punishment for sin but the assumption of sin itself. He explains,

> "The necessity whereby Christ had to go down to Hades lies not in some insufficiency of the suffering endured on the Cross but in the fact that Christ has assumed all the *defectus* [weaknesses] of sinners. God is solidary with us not only in what is symptomatic of sin, the punishment for sin, but also in co-experiencing sin, in the *peirasmos*

---

[8] This is the point made by Jean-Luc Marion in his essay "Evil in Person." The experience of evil is unavoidable and drives the subject from communion, toward casting blame, proclaiming their innocence. See Jean-Luc Marion, *Prolegomena to Charity*, trans. Stephen Lewis, Perspectives in Continental Philosophy 24 (New York: Fordham University Press, 2002), 1–30.

[affliction] of the very essence of that negation—though without 'committing' (Heb. 4,15) sin himself."[9]

In other words, the solidarity that Jesus expresses in the cross must be reflected in the loss of communion and the solitude of this loss. Under normal circumstances we experience solidarity as sharing with someone, being with someone, or sharing their circumstances. In this case, humanity in Sheol is alone, deprived of communion with all others. As a result, Christ's solidarity with humanity is a co-experience of being "self-enclosed," a solidarity that "excludes a communication on his part as subject."[10]

According to Balthasar, Christ's experience of hell is both unique and identical to that of humanity. The divine Son is personally the locus of communion between God and human beings. He experiences the isolation of each resident of hell. Humanity's rejection of God and of others registers directly in his person and he experiences every rejection and experience of rejection as his own. The Son's *human* experience of hell is, therefore, existentially identical to the experience of those who experience complete rejection. It is their experience assumed, and compounded. Yet Balthasar insists that Christ also experiences hell uniquely. As the locus of communion between God and human beings, only he can experience hell in its fullness, as the total human refusal of communion.[11] *Within* himself, he contemplates hell-in-itself, experiencing himself as the absence of communion.

---

[9] Balthasar, *Mysterium Paschale*, 137.
[10] Ibid., 164.
[11] In Balthasar's understanding, humanity's rejection of God creates a negative distance between creature and Creator. Christ experiences sin as a substantial reality generated by human freedom, or as the "effigies" of human actions gone wrong. For Balthasar human freedom is not nothing. It is real and has real consequences. Significantly, these consequences can only be "measured" by God

The Solidarity of Christ with Humanity in Hell

Balthasar has developed a very dark Christology indeed. To stop here would be to despair at death without resurrection. Hope emerges, however, through the solidarity of Christ with humanity in hell. On the cross, Christ is solidary with those who suffer. In hell, he becomes solidary with a humanity without possibility of communion. By assuming the existential condition of humanity, Christ assumes what is contrary to God. Balthasar explains that Christ's obedience—the obedience which constitutes his identity as the Son— "takes the existential measure of everything that is sheerly contrary to God, of the entire object of the divine eschatological judgment, which here is grasped in that event in which it is 'cast down.'"[12]

If you recall, Balthasar's Trinitarian theology indicates that persons of the Trinity are eternal acts of loving relation. In the descent to hell, the Son obediently enters into the absence of communion, and therefore experiences his self-negation. Paradoxically however, the Son's sharing in the creaturely NO manifests the very character of God's self-giving love. He inhabits our rejection of relation by being an absolute YES to relation. Thus, Christ's obedience to the Father "englobes" human isolation within the Triune relation.[13] Christ redeems humanity, *not by dying in our place*, but by *opening death to eternal life*, and earthly life to a "death to self." With his descent into finite suffering and death Christ transforms these realities into participations in the eternal

---

himself. Christ encompasses these depths of human sin, such that Hell is a function of the Christ event. Ibid., 172.

[12] Balthasar, *Mysterium Paschale*, 174.The reality of human rejection which is measured and judged in Christ is Hell. It is his obedient descent into the consequences of human freedom which makes Hell a reality for humanity, a reality which we only experience in and with Christ. Ibid., 178.

[13] Ibid., 82.

act of self-donation that is the life of God. Through Christ's solidarity, humanity is able to "die with Christ" into the activity of self-offering that *is* eternal life.

In summary, Balthasar's image for the Christ's descent to the dead is not the traditional victorious entrance into Sheol. The descent into hell is conclusion of a process by which the Son is immersed in the human experience of God-abandonment and absence of communion. The solidarity of God with humanity occurs precisely in the moment when the Son is most dehumanized, that is, by experiencing the loss of communion with all others. Yet Balthasar imagines that the site of death is transformed into life. Paradoxically, Christ's experience of hell is a manifestation of the Son's eternal act of giving himself to the Father. Thus, the Son's total identification and experience of depersonalized humanity is simultaneously a revelation of the eternal glory of the Divine Persons. By sharing in the absence of communion, Christ brings about communion.

The Site of Glory

For Balthasar, Christ's experience in hell is *existentially* identical to that of humanity, and that Christ's experience is transformed into the revelation of God's love. The solidarity of Christ secures the common existential situation between God and human beings. By implication, the experience of hell (or hell on earth) is already joined to the revelation of God's love. The darkest places of God-abandonment can be transformed into theophanies of God's glory. As a result, Balthasar provides the Christological and Trinitarian grounds for *identifying* the experience of the suffering, the dehumanized, and the god-abandoned with the glory of God.[14]

---

[14] We have not elucidated precisely what kind of *identification* can be made between human suffering and divine glory. Nor have we elaborated the

Unfortunately, Balthasar did not develop the concrete implications of his understanding of solidarity of Christ with humanity or connect his reflection on Holy Saturday with any concrete circumstance. Yet, Balthasar's reflections on the descent into hell in *Mysterium Paschale* suggest that his theological aesthetics and Christology may fruitfully be appropriated and corrected for contextual theologies, especially those that consider the situation of the oppressed. A theological optic similar to Balthasar's is found within James Cone's *The Cross and the Lynching Tree*, which narrates the transformation of vicious oppression into the privileged site of God's glorious revelation.

II. Cone on the Crucified and the Lynched

While Balthasar elaborates the Trinitarian dimensions of suffering as glory, James Cone elaborates the anthropological dimensions of this optic. Cone's *The Cross and the Lynching Tree*, inspired by the experience of the black church, draws the close parallel between the image of Christ on the cross and the victim of mob violence.[15] Cone's conclusions do not rest with the obvious analogies between the cross and lynching. Meditating on the salvific significance of the cross, he makes the provocative suggestion that the bodies of the lynched are the privileged medium of God's glory.

Cone did not easily arrive at this conclusion. As described in *The Cross and the Lynching Tree*, he was reticent to approach the subject of lynching head on. As a terrible symbol of white

---

connection in Balthasar's work between divine "glory," the glory of the Cross, and the human participation in this glory. While beyond the scope of this article, we recognize that these themes in Balthasar's theology are significant for suggesting how human suffering can be, in some sense, a medium of divine revelation.

[15] James H. Cone, *The Cross and the Lynching Tree* (Maryknoll, NY: Orbis Books, 2011).

supremacy, it triggered painful emotions.[16] Moreover, the correlation between the cross—which represents salvation—and the lynching tree, ran against the grain of his previous Christology. His previous interpretation of Jesus emphasized the liberation of the poor and oppressed.[17] The image of salvation as a liberation from racism and oppression is not easily reconciled with an image of salvation through the suffering on the cross. Cone was suspicious of those atonement theologies that envisioned the cross as the juridical requirement of sin and encouraged those who were suffering follow the example of Jesus and to passively accept their condition.[18]

The spirituals and black preaching provided avenue for Cone to reassess the meaning of the cross in light of the lynching tree. Although the "cross too often functions to make the oppressed accept their lot as God's will, this is not always the case. Notable exceptions include the slave spirituals which are full of references to the cross and suffering of Jesus."[19] The recovery of the theological imagination of the black church allowed Cone to reevaluate the meaning of the cross. This theological imagination claims the cross of Christ as its own, "[relating] the message of the cross to [its] own social reality."[20] Cone argues that, for the black church, the salvific significance of the cross of Christ is glimpsed through the experience of lynching and that the cross provides the means to theologically interpret lynching.

---

[16] Ibid., xiii.
[17] James H. Cone, *A Black Theology of Liberation*, C. Eric Lincoln Series in Black Religion (Philadelphia: Lippincott, 1970); James H. Cone, *God of the Oppressed* (New York: Seabury Press, 1975; Maryknoll, NY: Orbis Books, 1997). Citations are to the Orbis edition.
[18] After reading womanist criticisms of atonement Christology, Cone states, "It has been difficult for me to write and speak about the salvific significance of Jesus' cross." Cone, *God of the Oppressed*, xvi.
[19] Ibid., xvii.
[20] Cone, *The Cross and the Lynching Tree*, 158.

The question arises as to why the theological imagination that links lynching and the cross is significant. "Why bring that up? ... isn't that best forgot?"[21] Lynching is certainly an atrocity, but the lynch mobs are something of the past, right? Cone responds on several levels to this question. First, he recognizes that the specter of lynching continues to affect the imagination of black Americans. He states, "The trauma of lynching lives on in the blood and the bones of black people."[22] It is painful to recall the lynching of the past precisely because they impinge upon the meaning of the present: the ever-present possibility of grave injustice and barely-imaginable violence without recourse. Black Americans keenly recognize that, while great progress has been made in the last one hundred years of American history, there remains a violent racial tension bubbling just below the surface.[23] Second, whether or not one feels insulated from violence, lynching is branded onto black identity like the Shoah is branded onto Jewish identity. In light of these horrors, how is it possible to believe in a loving God who takes care of his people? "How can one believe that God loves black people in a world defined by 400 years of white supremacy?"[24] The experience of black people in the Americas demands a theological explanation of the experience of evil, a theodicy in some form. Third, Cone suggests that facing the reality of lynching with a theological lens is critical to doing God's will, that is, to overcome racism and mutual suspicion.

---

[21] James H. Cone, "Strange Fruit: The Cross and the Lynching Tree" (presentation, Ingersoll Lecture, Harvard Divinity School, Cambridge, MA, October 19, 2006), http://www.hds.harvard.edu/multimedia/video/strange-fruit-the-cross-and-the-lynching-tree.
[22] Ibid.
[23] See Bryan N. Massingale, *Racial Justice and the Catholic Church* (Maryknoll, NY: Orbis Books, 2010), 4–9.
[24] Cone, "Strange Fruit: The Cross and the Lynching Tree." Cone states that he has maintained a theological interest in the problem of evil since childhood. His first essay in college was entitled "Why Do People Suffer?" Cone, *The Cross and the Lynching Tree*, 153.

The Theological Syn-Optic

Leon F. Litwack mentions that lynching was an extrajuridical punishment used most frequently against whites (not blacks) during the nineteenth century in the West and Mid-West. Beginning in the 1890s it became a ritualized form of terrorism against black populations. "What was strikingly new and different in the late nineteenth and early twentieth centuries was the sadism and exhibitionism that characterized white violence...To kill the victim was not enough: the execution became public theater, a participatory ritual of torture and death, a voyeuristic spectacle prolonged as much as possible (once for seven hours) for the benefit of the crowd."[25] Lynching was thoroughly religious. The lynched was a "scapegoat," as René Girard calls it, the sacrificial victim rejected and killed by society in order to keep violence outside society.[26] While lynching was triggered by an accusation of wrongdoing by the victim, it was a form of public expiation of sin.

Given the religious nature of lynching in America, it is not entirely surprising that blacks interpreted lynching religiously. But given the experience of being on the receiving end of domestic terrorism, it is remarkable that "black people embraced the Christian cross that whites used to murder them."[27] As Cone shows, it is significant that the black church spontaneously interpreted lynching in terms of the suffering of Christ. Jesus was tortured and killed outside the city in a public spectacle. His victimhood is linked to the temple sacrifice of the Jewish high priest in the book of Hebrews. By joining the image of lynching to the image of the

---

[25] Leon F. Litwack, "Hellhounds," in *Without Sanctuary: Lynching Photography in America*, ed. James Allen (San: Twin Palms Publishers, 2000), 13.

[26] On the scapegoating mechanism and racism, see Susan Peppers-Bates, "The Satanic Nature of Racist 'Christianity," *The Journal of the Black Catholic Theological Symposium* 6 (2012): 45-71.

[27] Cone, *The Cross and the Lynching Tree*, 159.

cross, the black church responded to the narrative of the lynchers of black barbarity and criminality. The lynched, like Christ, was the innocent victim of a barbarous crowd. Likewise, the image of the cross responded to the expiatory role of lynching. The expiatory value of the blood of Christ provided a counter-narrative for the tortured flesh of the lynched. The cross of Christ reinscribed the religious meaning of lynching within a Christian framework and, as a result, highlighted the innocence of the victim and the closeness of the victim to Christ. For Cone, the historical absence of any significant theological reflection on lynching by white theologians and the failure of the white church to link these two realities is blindness, a failure to see correctly.

Cone suggests that there is more than an external analogy between the cross and the lynching tree. Despite the historical distance between the two, they are linked, not only in the religious imagination, but in reality.[28] The black spiritual, "Were You There" illustrates the realism with which the crucifixion of Christ is experienced and made present.

> 'Were you there when they crucified my Lord?'... Now the 'were you there' was a rhetorical question. Black people were there. Through the experience of being lynched by white mobs, blacks transcended their time and place and found themselves existentially and symbolically at the foot of Jesus's cross, experiencing his fate.[29]

The symbolic linkage between the two is no mere construction. It is based, for Cone, on the recognition of an existential connection

---

[28] Cone writes, "the Cross of Jesus and the lynching tree of black victims are not literally the same—historically or theologically. Yet these two symbols or images are closely linked to Jesus' spiritual meaning for black and white life together." Ibid., 165.

[29] Cone, "Strange Fruit: The Cross and the Lynching Tree."

between Christ on the cross and the experiences of the tortured. Cone's express conviction—God was "present at every lynching in the United States"—is not an abstract reference to God's omnipresence.[30] Rather, it is the assertion that, properly seen, the cross and the lynching tree exist within *the same existential frame*.

Yet the critical question remains: in what sense are these two events, separated by time and space, conjoined in some manner ontologically? Cone's previous theological work, as J. Kameron Carter suggests, sought to overcome the "hiatus between 'who Jesus *was*' in the world of the scriptural witness and 'who Jesus *is*' now *pro nobis* [for us]... What is continuous between the Jesus of Scripture who *was* manifest in the history—or perhaps better, the histories—that Scripture records, and the contemporary Jesus, who *is* manifest in history's now?"[31] In other words, what is continuous between Christ's historical body and the ecclesial body of Christ today? If the syn-optic intuition of the black church is true, along with its ethical implications, the interior relationship between the two histories is of utmost importance for the justification of this intuition.

According to Carter, in his theological career, Cone moved from a methodological dependence on Karl Barth's *analogia fidei* [analogy of faith] toward the *analogia existentia* [analogy of existence] of Paul Tillich. Barth's *analogia fidei* was a resistance against identifying the Gospel with our limited thinking about God, against identifying God's revelation through Christ with creaturely truth or untruth. For Cone, the *analogia fidei* was a deconstructive instrument for the "unmasking" of racist ideologies. However, it was "difficult to articulate in Barthian terms...how creaturely truth participates in God's truth." The *analogia fidei* did not allow for

---

[30] Cone, *The Cross and the Lynching Tree*, 158.
[31] J. Kameron Carter, *Race : A Theological Account* (Oxford: Oxford University Press, 2008), 171.

understanding how the experience of the black church is a corrective to racist ideologies and how the existential situation of blacks can be revelatory. Cone's methodology shifted toward Paul Tillich's *analogia existentia*, that is, an analogy of existential situation that allows one to understand the humanity of Christ through experience of human beings. For Tillich, God is being-itself, the ground of being; all existing things participate in this ground. The *analogia entis* [analogy of being] suggests for Tillich that our minds do, in some way, participate in the intelligibility of God. As a result, human experience is a finite reflection of its ground, suggesting an inner relationship between human experience and the divine truth. In other words, Cone's shift in methodology secured space for creaturely truth to reflect the divine truth, for human experience to reflect divine revelation. Cone's methodological shift is significant for seeing how the experience of black people and of the black church can make present the divine revelation manifest in Christ.[32]

Significantly, Cone suggests that there are soteriological and aesthetic connections between the cross and the lynching tree. Going beyond the consideration that human experience can reflect the divine truth, Cone suggests that the rejected, tortured, and lynched are the loci for seeing the form of Christ. Recognizing this theological reality requires "another type of imagination...the imagination to relate the message of the cross to one's own social reality, to see that 'They are crucifying again the Son of God' (Heb. 6:6)."[33]

---

[32] A tension remains, however, between Barth and Tillich, manifest in Cone's statement: "The Gospel is transcendent and immanent, it is here and not here..." Cone, "Strange Fruit: The Cross and the Lynching Tree."
[33] Cone, *The Cross and the Lynching Tree*, 158.

> God transformed the lynched black bodies into the recrucified body of Christ. *Every time a white mob lynched a black person, they lynched Jesus.* The lynching tree is the cross in America. When American Christians realize that they can meet Jesus only in the crucified bodies in our midst, they will encounter the real scandal of the cross.[34]

Although Cone states that we need a kind of *imagination* to see lynching in the same soteriological frame as the cross, this imagination does not suggest a lack of realism. This religious imagination is seeing correctly by recognizing the truth of Christ's real presence in and "God's loving solidarity" with broken black flesh.

To see aright is to recognize the paradoxical otherness of the crucified God *in* those subjected to torture and rejection. Cone elaborates:

> The Gospel is the Word of the Cross, a lynched Word...a tortured Word, a Black Word... The Cross and the Gospel cannot be separated. The cross stands at the center of the Gospel....The Gospel is a tortured word...the cross stands at the center of the Gospel...the heart of Christian mystery. Jesus died like lynched black victim...on the tree of shame.[35]

According to Cone, the Gospel overturns the values of this world. It is "suffering love" that stands at the heart of the Gospel. Because of Christ's historical sacrifice, complete rejection and total suffering are now essential to the revelation of the tortured Word. The bodies of the crucified constitute the means by which we encounter the Word.

---

[34] Ibid.
[35] Cone, "Strange Fruit: The Cross and the Lynching Tree."

The soteriological dimension of the cross and the lynching tree is closely related to the aesthetic dimension. In what sense can the unspeakable experience of the lynched be redeemed? Salvation, for Cone, is not merely a pleasant afterlife that makes up for the hell of this life. History must be saved from the inside. Cone's assertion of an interior, soteriological connection between the cross and the lynching tree responds to the scandal of evil. The cross of Jesus, he explains, *redeems* the lynching tree, redeeming the very rejection and suffering of the black body:

> The cross and the lynching tree need each other... The cross can redeem the lynching tree, and thereby bestow on lynched black bodies an eschatological meaning for their ultimate existence. The cross can also redeem white lynchers and their descendants. But not without a profound cost, not without a revelation of the wrath and the justice of God which executes divine judgment with the demand for repentance and reparations as a presupposition of divine mercy and forgiveness.[36]

This quotation reflects the realism with which two events are united somehow in fact and not only in the religious imagination. According to Cone, black spiritual imagination recognized the truth of the matter through a near-literal identification between or circumincession of the two.

In summary, the lynched are more than external analogies of the cross of Christ; they constitute icons of God's revelation of the Gospel to humanity, the ongoing communication of God's Word.[37] The failure to see Christ in those suffering is a failure to see Christ.

---

[36] Ibid.

[37] Cone extends his interpretation of lynching to those who suffer injustice through incarceration in American prisons, the death penalty, and torture as enemy combatants. Cone, *The Cross and the Lynching Tree*, 164.

Scandalously, for Cone, the lynched dead body is the locus of God's redemption and the site of God's glorious revelation. It is the place where we can see (with our eyes healed by God's grace) the truth of who God is. Though Cone himself does not fully justify the realism with which he understands the soteriological and aesthetic identification of these realities, he repeatedly mentions God's entrance into the human condition, God's *solidarity*, as the ground of this identification.

An Uneasy Tension

As mentioned above, Cone is uncomfortable with atonement Christologies that envision Christ's acceptance of the cross as a model for the oppressed to passively accept their suffering. Nevertheless, Cone's understanding of the cross and lynching tree and Balthasar's theology of Holy Saturday provoke the question: If human sufferers can be the media of divine glory, should we draw the conclusion that God wills suffering or oppression as part of the divine plan or as essential to the revelation of God's glory? If so, the result would be an unacceptable ethical imperative for the oppressed to passively accept their lot rather than to fight against oppression. Without attempting to resolve this delicate theological issue, we suggest a direction for approaching the problem by distinguishing between the kind of suffering entailed in communion with others and the kind of suffering resulting from the absence of communion.

Communion with God and human beings is God's will for us. Communion entails *kenosis*, giving or emptying oneself. However, communion should not be described as exclusively passive acceptance of violence or oppression. The authentic gift of self requires personal integrity rather than the dissolution of the self. It often requires active resistance in the efforts to change relationships and social conditions. The self-giving that establishes communion should be characterized primarily as something positive and essential to friendship, pleasure, and love. At the same time, in a fallen world, the gift of self is also a self-emptying that may be experienced as suffering. One must cease to be self-centered in order to enjoy friendship. The conversion from being self-centered to other-centered is a form of asceticism and may entail suffering. The old self must die—willingly and lovingly—in order to become the new self in Christ.

There is another kind of suffering that derives, not from communion, but from its absence. In loneliness, oppression, and violence, the person experiences the absence of communion. The absence of communion is a form self-enclosure that causes suffering. The ultimate suffering derives from lack of the ultimate good, communion with God. In itself, there is nothing salvific about this kind of suffering, for it is the closure of the self to every "other." It is a hell closed off to the presence of God. However, as Balthasar indicates, hell itself can be redeemed by the descent of Christ, transforming the place of suffering from death into life.

The intention of this article is not to propose the passive acceptance of evil as an ethical norm. Instead, we hope to indicate that the experience of horrific evil—itself not willed by God—can be transformed into the place of God's glory. Two truths are held in an uneasy tension. First, oppression and suffering are not willed by God, even as a means to a greater good. Second, those who are oppressed and experience suffering are solidary in Christ's redeeming action.

IV. Conclusion: God Revealed

There are considerable differences between the meditation on lynching by James Cone and the meditation on hell in Hans Urs von

Balthasar. While Balthasar's account of the descent only concerns the dead in hell, Cone's account of lynching concerns the hell experienced by the lynched and the effects caused by lynching on the living. Whereas Balthasar locates the fruition of Christ's solidarity (*kenosis*) in the descent to Sheol, Cone looks to the suffering on the Cross. The suffering endured in the Second World War and the Shoah is conspicuously missing from Balthasar's account of hell. Cone, on the other hand, seeks to apply a theological lens directly to the phenomena of lynching in the United States. Where Balthasar leaves undeveloped the implications of his meditations on the solidarity of Christ, Cone's work suggests a lens for recognizing God's glorious revelation in the midst of disaster. While Cone asserts a soteriological connection between the cross and the lynching tree, Balthasar's theology of Holy Saturday supplies a needed theological aesthetic.

Although they approach Christology from different directions, both Balthasar and Cone elaborate a theology in which the very site of suffering and rejection becomes the transparent medium of God's revelation. Without compromising the historical distance between the cross and the lynching tree, or the difference between divine and human sufferers, Cone and Balthasar indicate that Christ shares in the identical experience of those cut off from communion and abandoned. Flemister's *The Mourners* presents a lynching within the same frame as the Pietà and suggests, in the pose of the observers, an indeterminacy between mourning and praise. Similarly, Cone and Balthasar supply a theological lens for recognizing God's glory in those who suffer. As a result, the lynched, dead body is not merely analogous to the cross. It is a theophany that bears us into the very mystery of God's love. In the broken bodies of the rejected that the veil is torn, our eyes are opened, and we can say "Truly, this was the Son of God!" (Matt. 27:54).

WORKS CITED

Balthasar, Hans Urs Von. *Mysterium Paschale: The Mystery of Easter*. San Francisco: Ignatius Press, 2000.

Carter, J. Kameron. *Race : A Theological Account*. Oxford: Oxford University Press, 2008.

Cone, James H. *A Black Theology of Liberation*. C. Eric Lincoln Series in Black Religion. Philadelphia: Lippincott, 1970.

———. *God of the Oppressed*. Maryknoll, NY: Orbis Books, 1997.

———. "Strange Fruit: The Cross and the Lynching Tree." Presentation of the Ingersoll Lecture, Harvard Divinity School, Cambridge, MA, October 19, 2006. http://www.hds.harvard.edu/multimedia/video/strange-fruit-the-cross-and-the-lynching-tree.

———. *The Cross and the Lynching Tree*. Maryknoll, NY: Orbis Books, 2011.

Litwack, Leon F. "Hellhounds." In *Without Sanctuary: Lynching Photography in America*, edited by James Allen, 8–37. San: Twin Palms Publishers, 2000.

Marion, Jean-Luc. *Prolegomena to Charity*. Translated by Stephen Lewis. Perspectives in Continental Philosophy 24. New York: Fordham University Press, 2002.

Massingale, Bryan N. *Racial Justice and the Catholic Church*. Maryknoll, NY: Orbis Books, 2010.

Morgan, Stacy I. *Rethinking Social Realism: African American Art and Literature, 1930-1953*. Athens, GA: University of Georgia Press, 2004.

Pramuk, Christopher. "'Strange Fruit': Black Suffering/White Revelation." *Theological Studies* 67 (2006): 345–377.

The Representation of Blacks and Hispanics in Media Depictions of The Catholic Church

Sven Smith
Stetson University

Naseer Malik[1]

Fifty years ago, Pope Paul VI promulgated the <u>Decree on Means of Social Communication</u> at the end of the second session of the Second Vatican Council.[2] In this document, the Council outlined the responsibilities of the media in the rapidly-changing post WWII global society. Here, Smith and Malik present the results of an empirical study of the media's approach to the retirement of Pope Benedict XVI and the election of Pope Francis I. They show that the media reinforces stereotypes of the U.S. Catholic Church as a white institution by choosing to over-represent Catholic membership as well as leadership as overwhelmingly white, and by under-representing Black and Hispanic membership and leadership. In their fascinating interpretation of this study's significance, they find that White Catholics may blame institutional factors for our society's racial inequalities, but these same White Catholics are blind to the fact that the Catholic Church, as an institution, actually plays a role in perpetuating racial inequalities.

Representations of racial and ethnic minorities in the media have been overwhelmingly negative throughout most of American history, but they have also been underrepresented in the media, i.e., they are depicted in lower than their actual proportions in

---

[1] Naseer Malik earned his Master's Degree in Sociology at The University of Chicago in 2006.
[2] "Decree on Means of Social Communication," *II Vatican Council, October 11, 1962 – December 8, 1965,* accessed September 14, 2013, http://stjosef.at/council/.

society. When they are represented, the media depicts Hispanics and Blacks as negative or powerless while portraying Whites as positive and powerful. This may not be limited to broadcasts regarding secular sources. Although approximately one third of the U.S. Catholic membership consists of Blacks and Hispanics, in-depth coverage of minority opinion on television news may not reflect this proportion.[3] In this study, we sought to determine if the discrepancy in representation of racial and ethnic minorities extended beyond secular sources. If so, it could affect the way Catholics and non-Catholics view the Catholic Church and its relationship with racial and ethnic minorities. For example, the overwhelming depictions of Whites acting as leaders in the Catholic Church on television news may guide viewers to believe that Church leadership is dominantly White and that White leadership is a Church value, which is inconsistent with Catholic social teachings on the sin of racism.[4]

Media Influence on Viewers' Perception of Reality

Empirical literature suggests that media coverage is a strong determinant in the viewers' understanding of other persons. The more time a viewer spends with particular television portrayals, the

---

[3] Several studies have compared racial and ethical representation in media. Consistently, Blacks and Hispanics have been portrayed as culprits while Whites are shown as victims and/or 'heroes'; see R. Entman, "Blacks in the News: Television, Modern Racism, and Cultural Change," *Journalism Quarterly* 69 [2] (June 1992): 341-361; J.V. Turk, J. et al., "Hispanic Americans in the News in Two Southwestern Cities," *Journalism Quarterly* 66[1](1989): 107-115; and D. Romer et al., "The Treatment of Persons of Color in Local Television News: Ethnic Blame Discourse or Realistic Group Conflict," *Communication Research* 25[3] (June 1998): 286-305.
[4] "Poverty and Racism: Overlapping Threats to the Common Good," *Catholic Charities USA*, last modified 2008, accessed September 11, 2013, http://develop.wikispaces.com/file/view/Poverty+and+Racism+Overlapping+Threats+to+the+Common+Good.pdf.

more likely they are to believe them.[5] The greater the quantity of programs presented, the more the depiction is believed by the viewer.[6] These portrayals do more than just present information; they also allow viewers (including Catholics) to draw inferences about reality. The more this inaccurate portrayal is perpetuated in the media, the more likely the underrepresentation of Blacks and Hispanics is going to influence perceptions of the membership and leadership of the Church.[7]

In this paper, we present a brief history of media perceptions regarding the representation of racial and ethnic minorities. We then describe our research on the depictions of Blacks and Hispanics during the unusual circumstances of Pope Benedict XVI's retirement and the election of Pope Francis I. Finally, we discuss these findings along with other relevant literature, and suggest what these may mean for Blacks and Hispanics in the Catholic Church.

Highlighting Specific Groups in Media

Media—especially television—is often the only regular source of information Whites have about racial and ethnic minorities; the images are often negative and minorities rarely have the ability to influence how they are portrayed. Local news and other broadcast video-based media have long reified racial and ethnic groups as powerless, if they are portrayed at all. Ethnic minorities are severely underrepresented in television programming, and when they do appear, their prestige, power level, and ultimately social

---

[5] R. Akers and C. Sellers, *Criminological Theories: Introduction, Evaluation, and Application* (Oxford Press, 2012).

[6] G.J. Gorn, M.E. Goldberg, R.N. Kanungo, "The Role of Educational Television in Changing Intergroup Attitudes of Children," *Child Development* 42 (1976): 277-280.

[7] M. B. Oliver, "Portrayals of Crime, Race, and Aggression in 'Reality – Based' Police Shows: A Content Analysis," *Journal of Broadcasting and Electronic Media* 38, [2] (1994): 179-92; R. Entman, op. cit.

status are significantly lower than Whites'. This polarizes these groups from the majority group. Repeated portrayal of this power imbalance, even when based in reality, reinforces stigmatized popular perceptions about Blacks and Hispanics as well as identity formation for members of these groups.

News and media tend to reinforce the interests of dominant groups and symbolically reproduce and reinforce current social orders and institutions. The media has been depicted as an agent of oppression and as alienating Blacks from rightful inclusion. This segregation is further shown in the news media's preference for Whites, who have structural (institutional) advantages.[8] Noam Chomsky asserted that the very purpose of the media is to defend the agendas of privileged groups and reify the image of minorities as criminals and welfare leeches.[9] Expecting the media to behave differently is unrealistic, especially when the privileged groups are the rich and generally belong to the majority culture. Chomsky explained that it would be like counting on business to not be selfish but altruistic.

News and other media create in-group cohesion for the elite and maintain dominance over minorities. Minorities are often represented as stereotypes in either passive roles as the mere targets of decisions and actions or as breaking norms and laws, being deviant and a threat to the white audience, while Whites are represented as victims or as taking vigorous action against such deviance, placing themselves in the role of the hero. They are portrayed as defenders of the status quo and white cultural dominance. This repeated portrayal of racial minorities in a negative light contributes greatly to negative stereotypes, prejudices and ideologies, hence leading to the enactment and

---

[8] Chomsky, N. 1998. *The Common Good* (Tucson, Arizona: Odonian Press, 1998), 17 - 29.

[9] Ibid.

reproduction of racism. This is a trend that can be seen often and is predictable in the context of news programing.

Prominence of Papal Decision Gives Rise To This Study

In the few weeks leading up to and immediately following the election of Pope Francis I, hundreds of stories and interviews were aired by local network television news programs regarding Catholicism. Network news programs interviewed Catholics to provide information about Catholicism and Catholic life. In order to further broadcast to those interested in the vote, many of these stories were then uploaded onto the internet. The viewers of these news programs therefore constructed their views of the Catholic Church from these internet sources.

Watching the local and national news in March of 2013, we noticed that media coverage of all Catholics (but especially Hispanics) spiked when the discussion about the papal vote suggested that a Hispanic cardinal was being seriously considered for the papacy. This increase in coverage allowed for an opportunity to learn more about the participation of Blacks and Hispanics in the Catholic Church, and how their representation was portrayed in the media. In order to do this, we conducted an experiment designed to determine whether the portrayals of Black and Hispanic Catholics on television news differed from actual reality.

We sampled local news media depicting Catholics (Black, Hispanic, and White) available on the internet. These samples were divided in two ways. The first was a cultural group comparison, involving the three aforementioned groups. The second was a Membership versus a Leadership comparison, i.e. whether a person shown on TV news was represented as a member or a leader of the Church. We then looked at whether these depictions were representative of the actual demographics within the Catholic Church by comparing the television news depictions to those reported by Church authorities.[10]

In viewing network programming regarding Catholics and Catholicism, two questions emerged that this study seeks to answer:

(1) How does the local news coverage portray the racial/ethnic makeup of the Church?
(2) How does the depicted makeup compare to the actual racial/ethnic makeup of the Church?

We sought insights regarding these two questions by drawing distinctions between the following role-based depictions:

1) Interviews versus Showings (see Appendix B) any person shown in a news story who is not subsequently interviewed; and
2) Leaders versus Members (see Appendix B) (any person depicted as Catholic who is not shown in a leadership role).

---

[10] "Catholic Church in the USA," United States Conference of Cardinal Bishops: Church Diversity, last modified 2008, accessed May 21, 2013, http://uspapalvisit.org/backgrounders/index.htm; and "Intercultural Competencies," United States Conference of Cardinal Bishops: Cultural Diversity, last modified 2013, accessed May 21, 2013. http://www.usccb.org/issues-and-action/cultural-diversity/.

Hypotheses

Based on the research above, we decided to analyze the ethnic and racial representation of Catholics in the weeks surrounding the retirement of Pope Benedict XVI and the election of Pope Francis I. We formulated the following hypotheses:

1) Whites will appear on local news depictions of Catholics at higher rates than Blacks and Hispanics.
2) Blacks and Hispanics will be less likely than Whites to be portrayed as Leaders. When displayed, Blacks and Hispanics will be shown in positions that do not portray them as Leaders.
3) Blacks and Hispanics will be less likely than Whites to be the source for interviews.
4) The distribution of Catholics by race/ethnicity on television news will be inconsistent with the distribution reported by the Catholic Church and other authorities.

Methods

With use of a widely popular and utilized search engine, Google©, video excerpts of local news shows were downloaded from the internet in two different clusters:

1. Cluster A; 150 news excerpts extracted from the internet immediately following the retirement of Pope Benedict XVI on February 28, 2013. These were downloaded from March 2, 2013 to March 3, 2013.

2. Cluster B; 150 videos collected between March 15 and March 17, 2013, shortly following the announcement of 76-year-old Argentinian Cardinal Jorge Mario Bergoglio elected as Pope Francis I on March 13, 2013.

Regarding both Clusters, only local news broadcasts that were self-labeled with at least the following written content were kept and coded: "Pope", "local news" and "announcement."

A subsample was randomly drawn from both Clusters[11] to assure representativeness.[12]

Basic Variables of the Sample

Each cluster was then divided into two groups-(1) Showings and (2) Interviews. If there was a video representation of non-news personnel within the sample, this was counted as a "Showing". If non-news personnel were shown responding to a question posed to them by news personnel, this was counted as an Interview (see Appendix A). These two dimensions were further divided in two, resulting in a total of four variables: Interviews of Catholic Members, Interviews of Catholic Leaders, Showings of Catholic Members and Showings of Catholic Leaders (see the Tables 1-5).[13]

---

[11] 150 videos were drawn from each group. The units of each cluster were assigned a number from 1 to 300. Using a table of random numbers, each unit in the cluster was chosen based upon the last 3 digits in each number on a table of random numbers until 150 members were chosen from each cluster. This process serves as a check on unconscious or conscious researcher bias. Secondly, access to the body of probability theory that provided the basis for estimating the characteristics of the population, examining accuracy of samples, and ultimately generalizing the results of our sample back to the population.

[12] D. Kunkle, et al., "Violence in Television Programming Overall," in *National Television Violence Study: Scientific Papers 1994-1995*, edited by Media Scope, University of California Study, 1-171 (Studio City, CA: Media Scope, 1996); J. Potter, et al., "Content Analysis of Entertainment Television: New Methodological Developments," in *Television and Public Policy,* edited by J. Hamilton (Ann Arbor: University of Michigan Press, 1998), 55-104; B. J. Wilson, et al., "Violence in Television Programming Overall," *National Television Violence Study 3: Scientific Papers* (University of California Study, 1998), 3-204.

[13] Regarding Cluster A and Cluster B, only local news broadcasts that were self-labeled with at least the following written content: "Pope", "local news" and "announcement" were kept and coded. With regard to Cluster A, the additional word, "retirement" was used and with regard to Cluster B, the additional word, "election" was used. These additional words were used in order to narrow the scope and improve the primacy of the videos reviewed.

Only local news programs (e.g. programs that self-identify as "news") were coded, and all local news programs listed in the search results were eligible for inclusion in the clusters and ultimately the samples.[14]

Coding and Reliability

To ensure maximum reliability, only two coders reviewed the videos. "Coding" here is used to refer to the identification and grouping of the factors being measured (Showings, Interviews, Leaders, and Members). Each case was coded by both coders apart from each other, each unaware of the other's results. The codes of each were compared to look for inconsistencies. Coders identified the race/ethnicity of persons depicted, as well as their roles as Members or Leaders, and Interviews or Showings. Coder consistency in identifying each story was quite good, given the complexity of the task. Across all of the programs examined for reliability, both coders were highly consistent on the number of members and leaders stories, Hispanics, Blacks and Whites contained within the news programs. Overall, there was strong confidence in the accuracy of the data reported in the study (see Appendix A).[15]

---

[14] I.e. The internet news samples Clusters A and B, each with a total of 150 programs. If a repeat was found while proceeding through the content analysis, the second and any other multiple was dropped from the sample and the next number from the Table of Random Numbers was used to make the selection. If there was any problem with the video wherein it would not properly download or play, this same procedure was followed to ensure 2 samples of 150. However, when Cluster B was sampled, two copies were discovered that would no longer play given unknown problems with the Source. A total of 2 (1.9%) were removed from the sample because of downloading errors or other technical problems, yielding 148 programs for the sample drawn from Cluster B. No such problems were detected with the sample drawn from Cluster A.

[15] There was little variance between the two coders. Out of a total of 46 attribute assignments, the 2 coders were aligned 43 times. This yields a very high

RESULTS

Table 1: Members and Leaders and Showings/Interviews Compared by Group (n=298)

Race/Ethnicity	Leaders Showing	Leaders Interview	Total	Members Showing	Members Interview	Total
White	93% 269*	94% 88*	93% 357	91% 256*	85% 64*	90% 320
Hispanic	6% 17*	5% 5*	6% 22	7% 20*	12% 9*	8% 29
Black	1% 4*	1% 1*	1% 5	2% 5*	3% 2*	2% 7
Total	100% 290	100% 94	100% 384	100% 281	100% 75	100% 356

*reflects statistical significance at the .05 level. (n=298)

Comparisons of Depictions of Black, Hispanic, and White Catholics

Table 1 explains that there is a much greater depiction of White Catholics than Black and Hispanic Catholics in news stories available through the internet. Table 1 also shows that Leader depictions (including Interviews and simple Showings) are 71 times more likely to be White than Black, and 16 times more likely to be White than Hispanic.

Table 1 also shows the sums of Members depictions (including all three racial/ethnic groups). Member depictions were almost 11 times more likely to be White than Hispanic and more than 45 times more likely to be White than Black.[16] We conclude that there is a strong relationship between Race/Ethnicity and the Membership/Leadership depiction.

---

consistency (reliability) rating of 93%. See Appendix A for a more detailed explanation of the reliability tests.

[16] χ^2 (2, N = 298) = 57.17, p < .05. With this same alpha we computed chi-square statistics to determine whether these percentages were significantly different. An alpha level of .05 was used for all statistical tests. Since the P-value (0.0003) is less than the significance level (0.05), we cannot accept the null hypothesis. The statistics confirm that there is a strong correlation.

Comparisons of Interviews vs. Showings of Black, Hispanic, and White Catholics

Showings of Whites outnumbered those of non-whites by a factor of 10. In addition, White Members were interviewed 7 times more than Hispanics and 32 times more than Blacks as identified in Table 1. Depictions of Leaders followed a similar trend, with Whites outnumbering non-whites by a factor of 13. Leaders were 16 times more likely to be White than Hispanic, and 71 times more likely to be White than Black.[17]

Table 2A: Intra-Group Comparison of Leaders to Members for Clusters A and B (n=298)

	White Depictions	Hispanic Depictions	Black Depictions
Leaders	53% (n=357)	43% (n=22)	50% (n=5)
Members	47% (n=320)	57% (n=29)	50% (n=7)
Total	100% (n=677)	100% (n=51)	100% (n=12)

Table 2B: Intra-Group Comparison of Interviews to Showings for Clusters A and B (n=298)

	White Depictions	Hispanic Depictions	Black Depictions
Interviews	22% (n=152)	27% (n=14)	25% (n=3)
Showings	78% (n=525)	73% (n=37)	75% (n=9)
Total	100% (n=677)	100% (n=51)	100% (n=12)

Tables 2A and 2B are our intra-group comparisons. It is worth noting the differences between Leaders/Members versus the Interviews/Showings data. Table 2A shows complete White dominance, whereas Table 2B shows that, once depicted, Blacks

---

[17] X^2 (2, N = 298) = 245.23, p < .05.

and Hispanics are more likely to be in interviews than Whites. 27% (14) of all Hispanic depictions were Interviews. Similarly in the depictions of Blacks, only 25% (3) were Interviews. However, only 22% (152) of Whites were Interviews.[18] We recommend that this interesting and unexpected phenomenon be the focus of a future study.

Table 3: Depictions versus Actual By Race/Ethnicity for Cluster A and B (n=298)

	Depictions	Depictions		Actual	Actual
Race/Ethnicity	Members	Leaders	Total	Members	Leaders(Priests)**
White	90% 320	93% 357	677	61% 41.2m	91% 36,846
Hispanic	8% 29	6% 22	51	35% 23.6 m	8% 3,000
Black	2% 7	1% 5	13	4% 2.7m	1% 250
Total	100% 356	100% 384	741	100% 67.5m	100% 40,271

** Total number of priests – does not include lay leaders, deacons, bishops, or cardinals.

Comparison of Black, Hispanic, and White Catholics on Internet News to Records of the Catholic Church

After comparing Showings to actual membership parameters reported by literature and the Catholic Church (Table 3), it is evident that the internet news media depicted Whites in much greater than their actual proportions. Conversely, there is a smaller

---

[18] We computed chi-square statistics to determine whether these percentages were significantly different. Since the P-value (0.12) is greater than the significance level (0.05), we cannot reject the null hypothesis. However, the differences between Ethnic groups were all significant at .05 level.

percentage of Black members depicted than the actual membership. Although Blacks make up between 3% and 4% of Catholic parishioners, Blacks only made up 2% of the depictions. Similarly, Hispanics make up approximately 35% of Catholics in the United States, but only account for 8% of the depictions of members.

Depictions of Black, Hispanic, and White Leaders/Members Before and After Papal Selection.

The increase in Hispanic depictions between Clusters A and B was statistically significant, with three times as many showings and twice as many interviews in Cluster B than A. For Whites and Blacks, however, the differences between Clusters A and B were not found to be statistically significant.[19] There was an increase in Showings and Interviews for Blacks in Cluster B but this may be a function of the small number of Black depictions.

The increase in depictions of Hispanics is of special interest. Even though the percentages rise dramatically, they do not reach a rate comparable with the actual percentage of Hispanic Catholics in the United States (35%).

Table 4: Papal Retirement versus Papal Vote by Race/Ethnicity (n=298)

	Cluster A	Papal Retirement		Cluster B	Papal Vote	
Race/Ethnicity	Showing	Interview	Total	Showing	Interview	Total
White	96% 273*	94% 83	366	91% 252*	85% 69*	321
Hispanic	3% 9*	5% 4	13	10% 28*	12% 10*	38
Black	1% 2*	1% 1	5	3% 7*	3% 2*	8
Total	100% 286	100% 88	374	100% 276	100% 81	367

*significant at the .05 level.

---

[19] χ^2 (3, N = 298) = 57.83, p < .001

Table 5: Depiction of Actual Leadership Positions for US Catholics by Race/Ethnicity

	Total	Hispanics	Blacks	Whites
US Cardinals	100% 17[a]	0% 0	0% 0	100% 17
Active Bishops	100% 273[b]	11% 29[c]	4% 10[b]	85% 234
Total Priests	100% 40,271[d]	7% 3,000[e]	1% 250[a]	92% 37,021
Catholics by % Total Membership	100%	35%[a]	4%[a]	61%[f]

a "Catholic Church in the USA," United States Conference of Cardinal Bishops: Church Diversity, accessed May 21, 2013. http://uspapalvisit.org/backgrounders/index.htm

b "Intercultural Competences," United States Conference of Cardinal Bishops: Cultural Diversity, accessed May 21, 2013. http://www.usccb.org/issues-and-action/cultural-diversity/

c Center for Applied Research in the Apostolate, CARA Catholic Poll, Georgetown University, 2010.

d The Official Catholic Directory Anno Domini 2011. (P.J. Kenedy and Sons, 2011)

e Center for Applied Research in the Apostolate. The CARA Report, Summer 2012.

f Gautier, Mary L., and Mark M. Gray, "The Class of 2012: Survey of Ordinands to the Priesthood." Center for Applied Research in the Apostolate.

Review of Table 5 shows that Blacks are roughly 4% of the membership and 4% of the active bishops. However, Blacks are only 1% of the total priests and out of the 17 US Cardinals, not one is Black. Similarly, Hispanics are underrepresented in the media depictions as well Hispanics make up roughly 35% of the population of Catholic Members but only 11% of active bishops and 7% of total priests. They too are without any representation among the 17 US Cardinals.

Challenges

This research faced some obstacles worth noting. It is important to consider the possible lack of full registration of all U.S. Catholics and possible misinterpretation regarding Members/Leaders. Although each group was coded with a high level of reliability (consistency), the difference between depicted and actual Members/Leaders was determined only by visual aid as applied to the formal requirements laid forth in Appendix B. Also, Catholics depicted are compared to actual rates despite the fact that the persons shown in the videos may not have been registered Catholics. Second, traits among those depicted may not have been clear enough to determine completely accurately each person's race/ethnicity (Appendix B).

Hypothesis Confirmation

Our first hypothesis predicted that Whites would appear on local news' depictions of Catholics at higher rates than Blacks and Hispanics. This hypothesis was supported. As shown in Table 1, Whites, at 93%, were more likely than Blacks at 1%, or Hispanics at 6%, to be portrayed as Catholics on local news available on the internet.

Our second hypothesis predicted that Blacks and Hispanics would be portrayed in positions that would not display them as Leaders but as Members. This hypothesis was supported. To determine this we combined the Interviews and Showings for each group; this gave the sum of depictions for each race/ethnicity. We then compared the percentage of Leaders and the Members for each race/ethnicity, as seen in Table 2A. We combined the total numbers. Whites were the only group to have a greater number of depictions that portrayed them as Leaders rather than Members. Blacks were depicted roughly the same as Leaders and Members.

Our third hypothesis proposed that when comparing Showings versus Interviews within race/ethnicity, Blacks and Hispanics, when depicted, would be less likely to be displayed in Interviews than Whites. These figures are so similar across race/ethnicity, we conclude that there is no relationship between Race/Ethnicity and Interview percentages.

Our fourth hypothesis predicted that the ethnic distribution of Catholics on television news would be inconsistent with the distribution reported by the Catholic Church and other authorities. This hypothesis was supported.

Incongruity Between Actual and Expected Results

Hypothesis 3 claimed that, when comparing Interviews to Showings within each race/ethnicity, Whites would have a greater chance of being interviewed. This was not the case. The three ethnicities' ratios were relatively similar, with Hispanics being slightly more likely to be Interviewed (27%), than Blacks (25%), or Whites (22%).

With regard to Whites and Blacks, Depictions of the race/ethnicity of the Catholic Church remain roughly the same in the sample taken before (Cluster A) and the sample taken after the vote of the new Pope (Cluster B, see Table 4). This was not the case with Hispanics. It is important to note that the number of Hispanics depicted after the vote increased by 7%, but did not reach the actual percentage of Hispanics in the U.S. Church. Whatever effect the historical papal election may have had, it still did not bolster the Hispanic statistic to the point that the percentage of Hispanics depicted in Cluster B was equivalent to the actual percentage of Hispanics within Church.

Significance of Results for Catholic Church

The perceived race/ethnicity of American Catholics as shown on television network news shapes public perception of the racial ethnic composition of Catholics as a whole. If the Catholics interviewed in network news are only White then the public face of the Church is perceived to be overwhelmingly White. Viewers are likely to perceive the ethnic distribution of the Catholic Church by those people interviewed in television news programs. Underrepresentation of Blacks and Hispanics in television news creates an inaccurate perception by viewers. Approximately 35% of the Catholics in the United States are Hispanic. However, news media depicted only 8% Hispanic members, and 6% Hispanic leaders. Only 60-61% of the Catholics in the United States are White. However, an overwhelming 91% of Catholic depictions are of Whites. Similarly, 93% of the depictions of the Catholic Leaders (priests) are Whites. The trend in these numbers suggests that despite the actual disparity that exists in the Church, the depicted one far exceeds it! The same trend holds true for Member. There is a great overrepresentation of Whites when Catholics are depicted in the televised news media. The resultant underrepresentation of minorities is parallel with a preponderance of the literature confirming this exaggerated approach taken by the media.

Edgell and Tranby have suggested that Catholic parishioners believe that institutional factors in society play a major role in promoting racial/ethnic equality.[20] Using data from a national random sample telephone survey (n = 2081) conducted in 2003, they analyzed the effect of being Protestant, Catholic, etc., on social justice attitudes. They concluded that White Catholics share the

---

[20] Brian Froehle, "Sociology and the Catholic Church: Four Decades of Bitter Memories," *Sociological Analysis* 50, no. 4 (1989): 393-397.

opinion that laws and institutions explain Black disadvantage.[21] They stated:

> White Catholics are more sympathetic to explanations for African American inequality that place the responsibility on Whites, such as prejudice and discrimination, and with increasing religious involvement they are less likely to blame poor upbringing and more likely to believe that charities should do more to help.[22]

Edgell and Tranby further purport that this notion is paralleled by Hispanic Catholics. "Hispanic Catholics believe that laws and social institutions are a barrier ... to Black equality".[23] "Hispanic Catholics are especially likely to think that biased laws and social institutions are significant for explaining African American inequality".[24] This suggests that Catholics – at least the ones who participated in the survey – believe structural and institutional solutions are necessary to produce social justice.

Yet, the preponderance of the literature shows that most Catholics do not hold the Church to the same standard as suggested by Edgell and Tranby. Despite the fact that US Catholic Bishops declared racism to be a sin[25] and Catholic Charities USA © has formally stated that it must take action against racism,[26] scholars have pointed out that there is a lack of sensitivity or attention paid to the Black experience by the "Catholic moral

---

[21] P. Edgell and E. Tranby, "Religious Influences on Understandings of Racial Inequality in the United States," *Social Problems* 54, no. 2 (May 2007): 278.
[22] Ibid., 273.
[23] Ibid., 277.
[24] Ibid., 281.
[25] "Brothers and Sisters To US. US Catholic Bishops Pastoral Letter on Racism," last modified 1979, accessed September 11, 2013, http://www.usccb.org/issues-and-action/cultural-diversity/african-american/brothers-and-sisters-to-us.cfm.
[26] Poverty and Racism," op. cit.

guild."[27] Robert Bartlett described Black Catholics as "feeling the unwarmth" of the Catholic Church and perceiving the Church to be "lily white and cold."[28] Catholics are not including the Church as one of those charitable organizations or institutions expected to be an impetus for social justice. Our empirical findings buttress this notion of White privilege. They suggest a hegemonic structure that is, by its nature, unwelcoming to Blacks and Hispanics.

Media As Defeating Institutional Attempts Toward Balanced Representation

News media may also be discouraging racial/ethnic minorities to seek out the Catholic Church as a potential spiritual home. When local churches possess racial homogeneity, it may be intimidating for minorities to enter; and it also may attract more of the dominant group, Whites. Our own empirical findings further suggest that this disproportionality can be projected and even amplified by the media, furthering the chilling effect on the Church's current or potential Black and Hispanic membership. This repulsion of non-white would further sustain the news media's perception, which would be broadcast again to the viewers, creating a cycle in which minorities are even further discouraged.

Parallel to a preponderance of the previous research, our sampled media sources and our results portray a world where Whites hold most of the power and are necessary to establish order and to rescue minorities in trouble. This portrayal is supported by the relative social status of Whites and Blacks as well

---

[27] Bryan Massingale, "Racial Reconciliation In Christian Ethics: Toward Starting a Conversation," *The Journal of the Black Catholic Theological Symposium* 2 (2008): 50.

[28] Robert Bartlett, "Committed To The Faith While Sticking Out Like a Sore Thumb: Stories of Black Catholics on the Social Frontier," *The Journal of the Black Catholic Theological Symposium* 1 (2007): 92.

as the starkly divided depictions of Whites and minorities. It is the responsibility of television news reports to reign in their biases when retention and depiction of reality are requisites for proper communication.

Considering that the new Pope is Argentinian, the Catholic magisterium has taken an institutional step toward representative leadership. Despite this, the Church has a distance to travel before this is actualized, and local news is not pushing the Church toward equitable representation. This trend has been repeated in depictions of minorities in news regarding other areas beyond religion such as law enforcement, politics, and education; while Whites are consistently overrepresented in local news depictions available on the internet. Unfortunately, Chomsky's cynical position (that the press will not move beyond self-interest) is largely supported by the behavior of the news media during the Catholic campaign to reconfigure the Papacy.

Perhaps the only way to alter the underrepresentation of Blacks and Hispanics in news media is for the Church to ask a question. What might be the source for this inaccurate image? That source may be white dominance in Catholic leadership, a symbol of how the world, including media, perceives the Church. Encouragement of institutional practices that promote representativeness in membership, leadership, and depictions will foster a change in the perception by Catholics as well as non-Catholics (including non-Catholic media). If the leadership of the Church becomes more representative, or at least more minority apparent, it is reasonable to hypothesize that this noticeability will encourage media to become more balanced in its representations.

Americans take pride in the melting pot image of diversity. However, for Catholic Hispanics and Blacks, this image of harmonious acceptance and existence differs from their everyday experiences. While diversity and equality are ideals touted by many, Hispanics and Black Catholics will see that these concepts have yet to be fully realized in their Church leadership or the Church's portrayal in local media.

Underrepresentation And Its Import to Blacks

There are approximately 3 million Catholics[29] in the United States who are Black, making up approximately 4% of the total population of U.S. Catholics. However, only half of the actual Black Catholic proportion is visible in the depictions in our sample. 2% of the depictions of the Catholic leaders are depictions of Blacks. Yet, 4% of bishops in the US and 1% of the priests are Black. The trend in these numbers demonstrates an underrepresentation of Blacks in the news media.[30]

Blacks are often portrayed in situations that hinder their credibility both in the secular and non-secular world. Misrepresentation begets misrepresentation. In addition, when targeting a dominant White group concerning a topic believed to be associated with religious and moral piety, news media too often choose to not depict a group that is believed to be deviant and untrustworthy. The resultant overrepresentation of Whites heightens a sense of Whiteness as normative and more powerful, further serving the dominant racial/ethnic group.[31]

The audience, whatever their racial/ethnic origin, takes the media's depiction into a shared social construction of reality that is controlled by White perception. Portraying Black Catholics as

---

[29] "Demographics," U.S. Conference of Catholic Bishops, Secretariat for African American Catholics, last modified 2013, accessed May 23, 2013, http://www.usccb.org/issues-and-action/cultural-diversity/african-american/demographics/.

[30] D.A. Graber, *Crime News and the Public* (New York: Praeger, 1980).

[31] D. Kunkle, et al., op. cit.; J. Potter, et al., op. cit.; B. J., Wilson, et al., op. cit.

powerless supports the stereotypes shown in other aspects of news media. This perception of Black Catholics works with other depictions of Blacks to further reinforce stereotypes that extend far beyond the scope of the Church. This leaves Blacks to be viewed on the basis of the social reality constructed by Whites. Representation of Black Catholics in the media is important not only for Black Catholics but for all Blacks.

Looking Forward Given the Misrepresentation

There are a significant number of Black Catholics in the United States and throughout the world, each of whom represents possibilities for achieving the values of equality that the Church espouses. The Catholic Church is failing to properly utilize its resources as well as failing to enrich its leadership and overall membership.

Looking forward, it can only strengthen the Church to look for practical ways in which to implement the recommendations that this research suggests. The landscape of America has and continues to make drastic changes. Minorities will become the majority over the next 40 years. As an increasing number of minorities enter the fields of media and the Church, it is important that unique perspectives be added to the ongoing conversation of change, in order that the Church's values may be implemented in successful manner. Given the importance of these culturally diverse communities to Church success, it is imperative that these be represented at its administrative hierarchy in order to portray a more accurate Church to its members and non-members but also to better adjust and practically achieve its ideals in a culturally sophisticated and productive fashion. Exclusionary practice, whether actual or depicted, is never productive.

APPENDIX A: RELIABILITY TESTS

We checked our reliability using proportional reduction of error (PRE). The PRE technique used in this study is Lambda. Lambda is used as a measure of association appropriate for nominal data; it is a measure of the PRE which results from an association between two variables. It is the reduction of error divided by the original error. This means that, when two variables are related, the errors of predicting the values of one variable can be reduced by some percentage when we know the values of the other. It is the simplest of the PRE measures and most appropriate for this study given the number of coders (2) and the use of nominal data. The values of Lambda range between 0 and 1 with 0 signifying no PRE and 1 signifying total PRE.

Table 1A: Reliability Measure (Lambda) of Coders-(Race/Ethnicity)

			Coder 2		
	Race/Ethnicity	White	Hispanic	Black	Total
Coder 1	White	17	0	0	17
	Hispanic	1	2	0	3
	Black	0	1	2	3

Table 1B: Reliability Measure (Lambda) of Coders-(Leadership)

			Coder 2		
	Leader/Member	Leader	Member		Total
Coder 1	Leader	6	0		6
	Member	1	16		17

We wanted to measure the extent to which knowing Coder 1's assessments (the independent variable) can help us predict Coder 2's assessments (the dependent variable) in the race/ethnicity category as well as Leaders/Members distinction (reduction of error). We then compare this to our best guess regarding both (which we term original error). Therefore, the formula for the computation of this measure of association is: Lambda = PRE = reduction of error/original error. Table 1A (of this Appendix) shows the extent Coder 1 is similar to Coder 2 (and thereby can be used to predict Coder 2's code selection when determining Membership or Leadership.

Original Error (Error before knowing coder 2): We wish to make our best guess as to Coder 2's assessment of Membership/Leadership. The original error is discovered by examination of the "Totals" column. In this case there would be an identical chance that anyone in this sample made a "White," "Hispanic," or "Black" assessment. If one were to guess what type of assessment both coders made without knowing the definitions or identifications, it would be the same to guess any one of the three. The best guess here would be "White". It is probable that such a process would lead to 17 correct and 6 incorrect guesses. There would therefore be 6 original errors in Table 1a.

Improved Error (Error after): The reduction of error is discovered by examination of the results of the cross-tabulation. Knowing the attributes determined by Coder 1, improves the ability to determine what Coder 2 determined. We would be correct 21 times (17 + 2 +2 = 21) and wrong 2 (1+1+0=2) times. With the errors before = 6 and the errors after equaling 2, the improved error is 2.

We then reviewed the amount that Coder 1's attribute assignments associates with Coder 2's attribute assignments.

Reduction in error = errors before (6) - errors after (2) = 4. We compare this to the original number of errors: 4/6 = .66 = 66%

When considering race/ethnicity, Coder 1 can predict Coder 2 by a proportion of 66% better than if from random choice. In other words, Coder 1's association with Coder 2 (practically the training that both followed) has *reduced error* by a proportion of 66% from arbitrary coding. Overall, combining race/ethnicity and the Membership/Leadership errors to determine the overall reduction in error, we find:

Race/Ethnicity: Errors before = 6, Errors after = 2; Leadership/Membership: Errors before = 6, Errors after = 1. Therefore the Total Errors before = 12 and Total Errors after = 3

How *much* does Coder 1 associate with Coder 2? *Reduction in error* = errors before (12) - errors after (3) = 9. Ultimately, we compare this to the original number of errors: 9/12 = .75 = 75%

When considering the overall attribute assignment of both Coders' variable sets, the maximum training affect on Coder 2 has reduced error by a proportion of 75%. A PRE of 66% and 75% for both variable sets is strong direct indicator that the formalized definitions and identifications (Appendix B) used by the Coders were followed very similarly by both.

Appendix B: Definitions

Depictions. A video representation of a person within the sample set.

Identification of Race/Ethnicity. The following items were used to assess the race/ethnicity of those displayed over the media source: (a) video (visual), (b) identification of member by the media source, (c) photo shown. When these more apparent indicators of race/ethnicity were not available, it was inferred based on characteristics of the story. Two variables were used: (a) surname (e.g. Rodriguez is associated with Hispanic) and (b) prior news reports that indicate the same depicted person's race/ethnicity. This was used to err on the side of caution by allowing for the maximum number of minority counts.

Identification of Leadership/Membership. The following items were used to assess the membership of those displayed over the media source: (a) video, (b) identification of member by the media source, (c) photo shown. When these more apparent indicators of membership were not available, it was inferred based on characteristics of the story.

Interview. Those non-news personnel depicted as responding to a question posed to them by the reporter or Interviewer. If they did not appear as though they were responding to anything asked of them but were still making a statement, this was NOT included as an Interview. Cues for responding to an Interview included responding to a question, looking into a camera, and looking like they were pondering a question or statement posed to them before they spoke.

Leader. Leaders are defined as people displayed with those traits that indicate formal leadership in the Catholic Church. They must be displayed in such a manner that they are accompanied by two associations with leadership in the Catholic Church. These indicators can be auditory or visual. For example, in a video news story, if a person was depicted while Catholic Leadership is being discussed in a voiceover, this alone is not enough to code them as a Catholic Leader for our purposes. However, if the person is shown leading a congregation of Catholics or leading a group while wearing the garb that distinguishes them as a cardinal or bishop, then this was sufficient for the "Leader" designation. Only those persons designated by the media sources as leaders or as displaying behavior pertaining to leadership with the Church were coded as "Leaders".

Member. Members were defined as persons that are members, associates, and/or supporters of the Catholic Church. They must be displayed in such a manner that they are accompanied by two associations with the Catholic Church. In other words, each must possess at least two indicators suggesting they are members/supporters of the Catholic Church. These indicators can be auditory or visual. For example, in a video news story, if a person is depicted while Catholics are being discussed in a voiceover, this is not enough to warrant them as Catholic for our purposes. However, if that person is shown walking into a Catholic Church or wearing a Catholic symbol or holding a Bible, then this, in addition to the voiceover, would be more than one indicator and so, for the purposes of this research, would be coded as "Catholic".

Showing. A mere visual depiction of a person not being interviewed but merely displayed. It is any person shown that was not interviewed and not a Pope. Most Interviews were part of a story that included Showings of other persons not interviewed so it was common for stories to be coded as containing Interviews and

Showings after or before the Interviews. Interviews and Showings are mutually exclusive categories.

White and Other. The focus of this research is the representation of Blacks and Hispanics in relation to all other groups, Whites being the majority; the statistical categories for Asians and Native Americans, Pacific Islanders, Tahitian, etc. were categorized as the overarching "White and Other". It is important to note that this originally included a fourth category. From the entire sample 298 videos collected (2 being dropped) not one Local News broadcast of a Catholic Showing or Interview depicted the physical characteristics commonly associated with the Asian ethnicity.

WORKS CITED

Akers, R., and Sellers, C. *Criminological Theories: Introduction, Evaluation, and Application.* Oxford Press, 2012.

Bartlett, Robert. "Committed To The Faith While Sticking Out Like a Sore Thumb: Stories of Black Catholics on the Social Frontier." *The Journal of the Black Catholic Theological Symposium* 1 (2007): 84-107.

Catholic Charities USA. "Poverty In America Issue Brief, Poverty and Racism. Overlapping Threats To The Common Good. Last modified 2008. Accessed September 11, 2013. http://develop.wikispaces.com/file/view/Poverty+and+Racism+Overlapping+Threats+to+the+Common+Good.pdf.

Center for Applied Research in the Apostolate. "Frequently Requested Church Statistics." *The CARA Report,* Last modified 2013. Accessed September 11, 2013. http://cara.georgetown.edu/CARAServices/requestedchurchstats.html.

Chomsky, Noam. *The Common Good.* Tucson: Odonian Press, 1998.

Edgell, P and Tranby, E. "Religious Influences on Understandings of Racial Inequality in the United States." *Social Problems* 54, no. 2 (May 2007): 263-288.

Entman, R., "Blacks in the News: Television, Modern Racism, and Cultural Change," *Journalism Quarterly* 69, no.2 (June 1992) 341-361.

Entman, R., "Representation and Reality in the Portrayal of Blacks on Network Television News," *Journalism Quarterly* 71 (1994): 509-520.

Froehle, Brian. "Sociology and the Catholic Church: Four Decades of Bitter Memories." *Sociological Analysis* 50, no. 4 (1989): 393-397.

Gautier, Mary and Mark Gray. "The Class of 2012: Survey of Ordinands to the Priesthood." *Center for Applied Research in the Apostolate.* Last modified 2012. Accessed September 11, 2013. http://www.usccb.org/beliefs-and-teachings/vocations/ordination-class/upload/Ordination-Class-of-2012-Report-FINAL.pdf.

Gorn, Gerald, M.E.Goldberg, and R.N. Kanungo. "The Role of Educational Television in Changing Intergroup Attitudes of Children." *Child Development* 47 (1976): 277-280.

Graber, D. A. *Crime News and the Public.* New York: Praeger, 1980.

Hamilton, D, L., Stroessner, S. J., and Driscoll, D. M. "Social Cognition and the Study of Stereotyping." In *Social Cognition: Impact on Social Psychology*, edited by P. G. Devine, D. L. Hamilton, and T. M. Ostrom, 292–323. San Diego, CA: Academic Press, 1994.

II Vatican Council, October 11, 1962– December 8, 1965. "Decree on Means of Social Communication." Accessed September 14, 2013. http://stjosef.at/council/.

Kunkle, D., B.J. Wilson, D. Linz, J. Potter, E. Donnerstein, S.L. Smith, E. Blumenthal, and T. Gray. "Violence in Television Programming Overall." In *National Television Violence Study: Scientific Papers 1994-1995*, edited Media Scope, University of California Study, 1-171. Studio City, CA: Media Scope, 1996.

Oliver, M. B., "Portrayals of Crime, Race, and Aggression in 'Reality – Based' Police Shows: A Content Analysis." *Journal of Broadcasting and Electronic Media* 38, no.2 (1994): 179-92.

Massingale Bryan. "Racial Reconciliation In Christian Ethics: Toward Starting a Conversation." *The Journal of the Black Catholic Theological Symposium* 2 (2008): 31-58

Potter, J., D. Linz, B. Wilson, E. Donnerstein, D. Kunkle, S. Smith, E. Blumenthal, and T. Gray. "Content Analysis of Entertainment Television: New Methodological Developments." In *Television and Public Policy,* edited by J. Hamilton, 55-104. Ann Arbor: University of Michigan Press, 1998.

Romer, D., Jamieson, K. H., and De Coteau, N.J. "The Treatment of Persons of Color in Local Television News: Ethnic Blame Discourse or Realistic Group Conflict." *Communication Research* 25, no. 3 (June 1998): 286-305.

The Official Catholic Directory Anno Domini. Berkeley Heights, New Jersey: P.J. Kenedy and Sons, 2011.

Turk, J.V., Richstad, J., Bryson, R. L., and Johnson, S. M. 1989 "Hispanic Americans in the News in Two Southwestern Cities." *Journalism Quarterly* 66, no. 1: 107-115.

United States Conference of Catholic Bishops. "Pastoral Letter on Racism. Brothers and Sisters To Us." Accessed September 11, 2013. http://www.usccb.org/issues-and-action/cultural-diversity/african-american/brothers-and-sisters-to-us.cfm.

United States Conference of Catholic Bishops. "Catholic Church in the USA, Church Diversity." Accessed May 21, 2013. http://uspapalvisit.org/backgrounders/index.htm .

United States Conference of Catholic Bishops. "Demographics." Last modified 2013. Accessed May 21, 2013. http://www.usccb.org/issues-and-action/cultural-diversity/african-american/demographics/.

United States Conference of Catholic Bishops. "Intercultural Competences, Cultural Diversity." Accessed May 21, 2013. http://www.usccb.org/issues-and-action/cultural-diversity/.

U.S. Census. "Reported Internet Usage for Households, by Selected Householder Characteristics: October 2009." Accessed May 19, 2013. http://www.census.gov/hhes/computer/publications/2009.html.

Wilson, B. J., Kunkle, D., Linz D., Potter J., Donnerstein, E., Smith, S.L., Blumenthal, E., and Berry, M. "Violence in Television Programming Overall." *National Television Violence Study 3: Scientific Papers*, University of California Study (1998): 3-204.

Book Reviews

THE COLOR OF CHRIST: THE SON OF GOD AND THE SAGA OF RACE IN AMERICA, by Edward J. Blum and Paul Harvey. Pp. vi + 340. University of North Carolina Press, Chapel Hill, North Carolina, 2012. $32.50 (hardcover), ISBN 978-0807835722; and

CHRISTOLOGY AND WHITENESS: WHAT WOULD JESUS DO?, edited by George Yancy. Pp. xi + 224. Routledge, London and New York, 2012. $39.95 (paper), ISBN 978-0415699983.

In 1969, James H. Cone proclaimed that God is Black as is Jesus, the son of God. He was following in the footsteps of AME Bishop Henry McNeal Turner who, in 1891, proclaimed the same truth in the language of his time (God is a Negro). McNeal's proclamation received little attention but Cone's, presented in the midst of the civil rights and Black Power turmoil, landed like a bombshell in the hearts and minds of many, especially those in Christian seminaries and churches. Both blacks and whites were left grappling with a statement that as with all metaphors contrasted that which was seen as holy in its fullest sense with that which was not so seen, blackness and, thus, black people, and confounded their faith.

The two books under discussion address the issue of the skin color (as well as eye and hair color) of Jesus over the past 500 years as well as the significance of whiteness as a symbol of authority and privilege in the United States. The authors' use different perspectives and methodologies, history for Blum and Yancey and theology (Christology) and philosophy for the contributors to the Yancy volume but reach a similar conclusion: the perception of Jesus today is of critical importance in a world and faith (Christianity) that is increasingly one of persons of color.

In **The Color of Christ**, Blum and Harvey review 500 years of human history from the founding of the U.S. to the present day in order to discern how a Palestinian Jew was transformed into an Aryan /Nordic white, a symbol of power and domination for white Americans and the basis for claims that the U.S. is not only a Christian nation but it is also a white nation. Using art, history, cultural studies, religious history, and the interpretations of white, black, Native American, Latino/a, and Asian Christians in the United States, the authors explore how, in the United States, Jesus was initially seen only in a spiritual sense as a blinding or brilliant light or as a bloodied figure of suffering by iconoclastic Protestants. However, these images slowly and subtly shifted and Jesus came to be seen as a white European male, the nation's leading symbol of superiority and domination. This image of Jesus was repeatedly remade visually into a "sacred symbol of white Americans' greatest aspirations, deepest terrors, lowest actions, highest expressions, and mightiest strivings for racial power and justice" (2).

The image of Christ became a source of conflict over the centuries as each ethnic/racial group in the United States attempted to claim him as their own. Despite ongoing efforts by white Americans to depict Jesus in their own image and likeness in order to use him as a symbol of white power and white supremacy, others, persons of color, fought to preserve his universal appeal to all. Native Americans contested the whitening of Jesus as they saw him as a bloodied and battered co-sufferer while those of African descent who were enslaved also saw in him a co-sufferer who, even though he might be white, sided with them in their oppression rather than joining with slave masters and others to oppress them. It is not until the 1960s and after, however, that we find efforts to re-imagine Jesus as Black, Latino/a, Asian or Native American among others. This is because the westernized white image of Jesus had become the norm, deeply embedded in the psyche of all Americans regardless of race and ethnicity, aided and abetted by Sunday School depictions, artwork, especially Sallman's painting of *The Head of Jesus*, and a sustained propaganda effort that made the US the greatest purveyor of this image throughout the world.

As a result, "the body of Christ ascended from largely unknown and inconsequential" at the beginning of the nation's founding "to becoming an object of obsession, adoration, confusion, conflict and comedy by the Twenty-first century....the sacred [was] racialized and.... the spiritualization of race [gave] notions of human difference not only a life beyond scientific studies or anthropological insights but also a sense of eternal worth" (14-15). By linking Jesus with whiteness, all Americans were taught that whiteness was the norm and that white domination "was a God-given right" (15) unavailable to many.

The Color of Christ "shows how the body of Jesus rose from irrelevant to critical in American history, how the white Jesus became a dominant and unstable symbol of white American supremacy, how he was refashioned with changes to whiteness, and how millions of women and men of color put their faith in him while transforming him in subtle ways. It demonstrates how liberation theologies emerged first among everyday peoples and then among theologians. And, it explains how white Christ imagery has had the power to last and shape-shift even after massive assaults from civil rights crusades, scientific discoveries, and demographic transformations" (22).

George Yancy has brought together a diverse group of scholars to answer the critical question:"What would Jesus do?" looking through a lens of "whiteness." In this way, "the philosophical, ideological, and theological underpinnings of our racialized narratives and interactions" can be exposed and discussed (xiv). As Kelly Brown Douglas notes in her preface that the work "exposes the multiple ways in which 'whiteness' has acted as a 'transcendental norm', that is a standard for all that which is good and acceptable," and reveals the impact of 'normative whiteness' on bodies that aren't white, especially black bodies (xiv).

The question is raised: What is the meaning of "whiteness", not just for persons of color but even more importantly for whites themselves? The contributors in their responses do not seek a pietistic or overtly moral perspective but see the question of "what would Jesus do?" as one of social justice and Christian integrity. Yancy, himself, defines his understanding of whiteness as "a historical practice that continues to express its hegemony and privilege through various cultural, political, entrepreneurial, and institutional practices, and that forces bodies of color to the margins and politically and ontologically positions them as subpersons" (5). He and the other writers also acknowledge that "race is ontologically empty and epistemologically bankrupt," but as a "socially constructed category, race has real socio-ontological, existential, political and psychological implications for those categorized as non-white" (12).

Coming from diverse theological and philosophical disciplines as well as religious perspectives, some contributors use the understanding of Jesus as white as a way to explore his meaning in terms of sustaining normative whiteness and his relevance in pursuit of racial justice. Another group questions the significance of a black Christ in black faith and theology. Some argue that a black Christ is of critical importance for those whose blackness has been historically demonized while others find that image troubling, seeing it as "simply reinforcing the reality of whiteness while ignoring the web of power relationships which foster white supremacy" (xv). Yet another group of contributors question the relevance of Jesus for contemporary racial issues arguing that the issue of Jesus' skin color and action in today's world forces contemporary Christians to become "actively engaged in today's struggles for justice" (xv) while others disagree, arguing that humanity must wait until Jesus' actual return when he will provide a clear answer to his stance on race. Until then we must live in hope of the future where Jesus will render racism no longer conscious. One final group asserts that the question simply gives positive value to suffering and is thus detrimental to the ongoing struggle against injustice because of it.

As can be seen by the diversity of responses, there is no one clear or definitive answer; rather it is constantly evolving. Our answer is affected by and filtered through our own lived experiences of both Jesus and the world in which we live.

The central argument for the work is that looking through a "certain hermeneutic lens Christian theology and whiteness" can be seen as completely and totally "incompatible" (5) because Jesus Christ is love and that love is a refusal to accept whiteness. Christology is fundamentally predicated upon love, thus, any actions or ways of thinking that deny love are not Christian. White Christians must, therefore, reject whiteness while continuing to benefit from its power and privilege. "Christology becomes a deep existential prism through which to think about what ought to be done about one's whiteness and the problem of whiteness in our contemporary moment" (6).

Yancy calls for a metanoia that requires a "constant process of choosing against whiteness, training against whiteness and constantly offering a Christian anthropology that militates against whiteness as the quintessential image of God" (6). By asking what Jesus would do, white Christians are led to rethink their white Christian identities within "the context of Jesus' liberative praxis."

Both of these works break new ground in terms of their approaches and goals. *The Color of Christ* provides a detailed and in-depth review of Americans reception of Jesus as human and divine and the impact of the increasingly whitenized image that became normative. The authors clearly show the struggles that took place among the different racial and ethnic groups in the United States and how the whitening of Jesus played a foundational role in the emergence of the US as a nation. It resulted in laws that defined a person by race/ethnicity, especially their level of whiteness, rulings which were comparable both in social, legal and psychological effect to the apartheid laws of South Africa Seeing itself as a white nation grounded in the Christian faith and exporting its own biased understandings of race around the world, the United States as a result became a world power whose racial perspective affected everyone. It has left us with a legacy of race consciousness that significantly hinders our ability to come together as a nation united with a common goal.

Christology and Whiteness can be said to build upon this history to challenge the readers, whether religious scholars or laity, to rethink our own images of Jesus and to question what has influenced our image and understanding of Jesus the Christ. White Christians are challenged to encounter and grapple with their whiteness in ways that will, hopefully, enlighten them to the ways in which whiteness has served to uplift one group of Americans while demonizing others. The contributors provide an excellent exploration of the question with a diversity that challenges and informs.

Both books are well-written, informative, and revealing of the great dichotomy that still persists in the United States over the issue of race. We are called as readers to recognize our own failings and biases in order to free ourselves to work toward perspectives of Jesus that are compatible with and informed by the experiences of all. We are challenged to be aware of the weight and burden of whiteness that still oppresses not only in the United States but globally and to work toward newer and more inclusive understandings of our history and the many who contributed to it as well as to the critical role a Jesus of all the people can play in our lives.

One minor point of criticism with *The Color of Christ* is that they provided a number of images of Jesus over a historical timeline but the great majority (over two-thirds) still reflected white rather than Black, Latino/a, Asian or other images. It would have been helpful to have some of the many contemporary and beautiful images now portrayed in many Black and other churches to support the understanding that times are, indeed, changing.

Diana L. Hayes, Ph.D.
Emerita Professor of Theology
Georgetown University

CHRONOLOGY OF BCTS ANNUAL MEETINGS

2013 Bellarmine University, Louisville, Kentucky

2012 St. Thomas University, Miami Gardens, Florida

2011 Marquette University, Milwaukee, Wisconsin

2010 Stetson University, DeLand, Florida

2009 Atlanta University, Atlanta, Georgia

2008 Catholic Theological Union and Loyola University, Chicago, Illinois

2007 St. Meinrad Archabbey, St. Meinrad, Indiana

2006 Boston College, Boston, Massachusetts

2005 St. Mary's Seminary at the University of St. Thomas and St. Francis of Assisi Parish, Houston, Texas

2004 Xavier University, New Orleans, Louisiana

2003 Atlanta University, Atlanta, Georgia

2002 Gonzaga University, Spokane, Washington

2001 University of Dayton, Dayton, Ohio

2000 Marquette University, Milwaukee, Wisconsin

1999 University of Notre Dame, Notre Dame, Indiana

1998 Marquette University, Milwaukee, Wisconsin

1997	No meeting
1996	The University of San Diego, San Diego, California
1995	St. John University, New York, New York. Met in conjunction with ACHTUS (Academy of Hispanic Theologians in the United States)
1994	Mt. Vernon, Hotel, Baltimore, Maryland
1993	The Mexican American Cultural Center San Antonio, Texas
1992	Duquesne University, Pittsburgh, Pennsylvania
1991	The Atlanta University Complex, Atlanta, Georgia
1979	Second Meeting of the BCTS Motherhouse of the Oblate Sisters of Providence Baltimore, Maryland
1978	First Meeting of the BCTS Motherhouse of the Oblate Sisters of Providence Baltimore, Maryland

www.ingramcontent.com/pod-product-compliance
Lightning Source LLC
Chambersburg PA
CBHW071436160426
43195CB00013B/1927